Wild Animals

Coloring Book

Allpress Publications

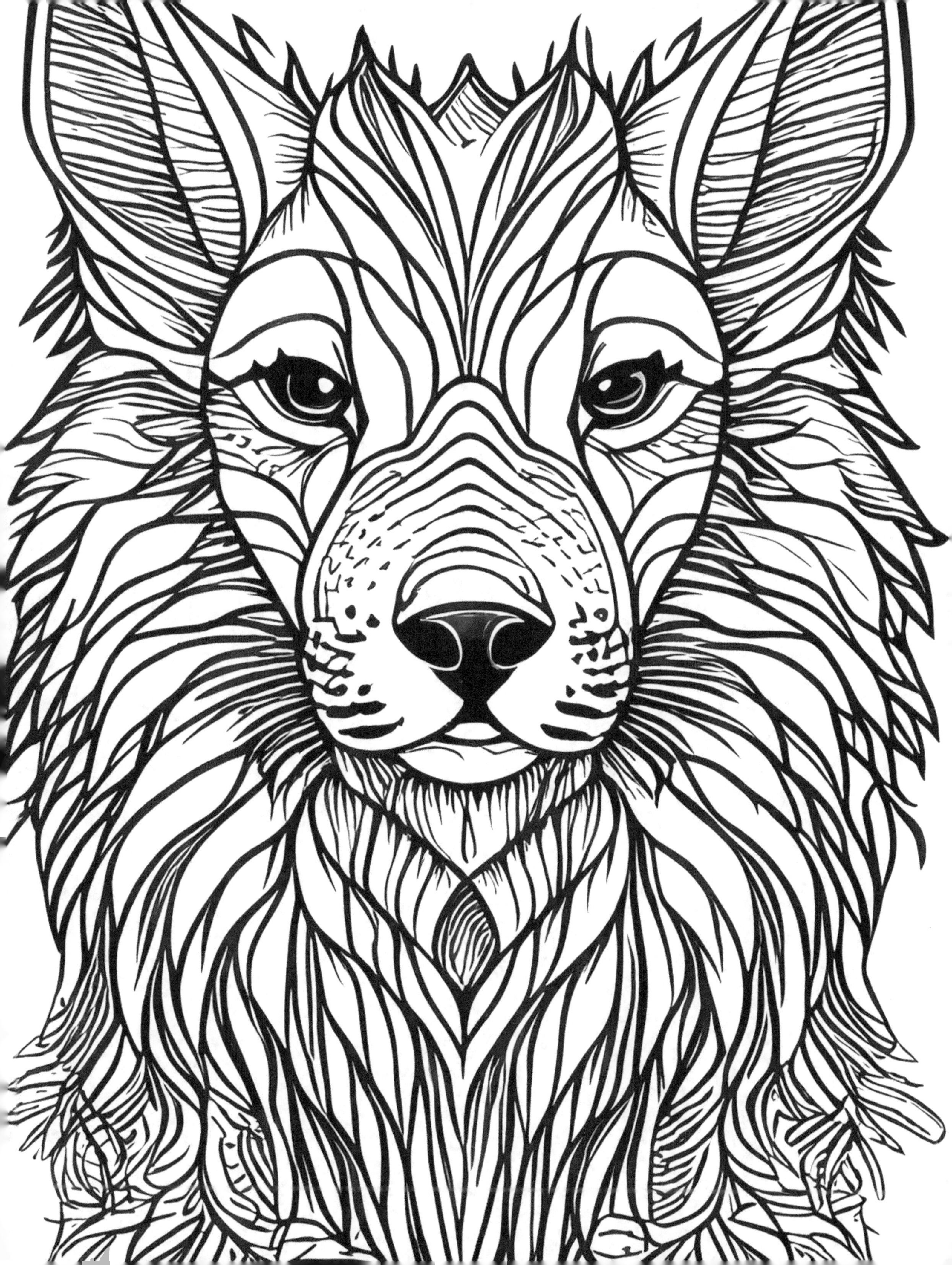

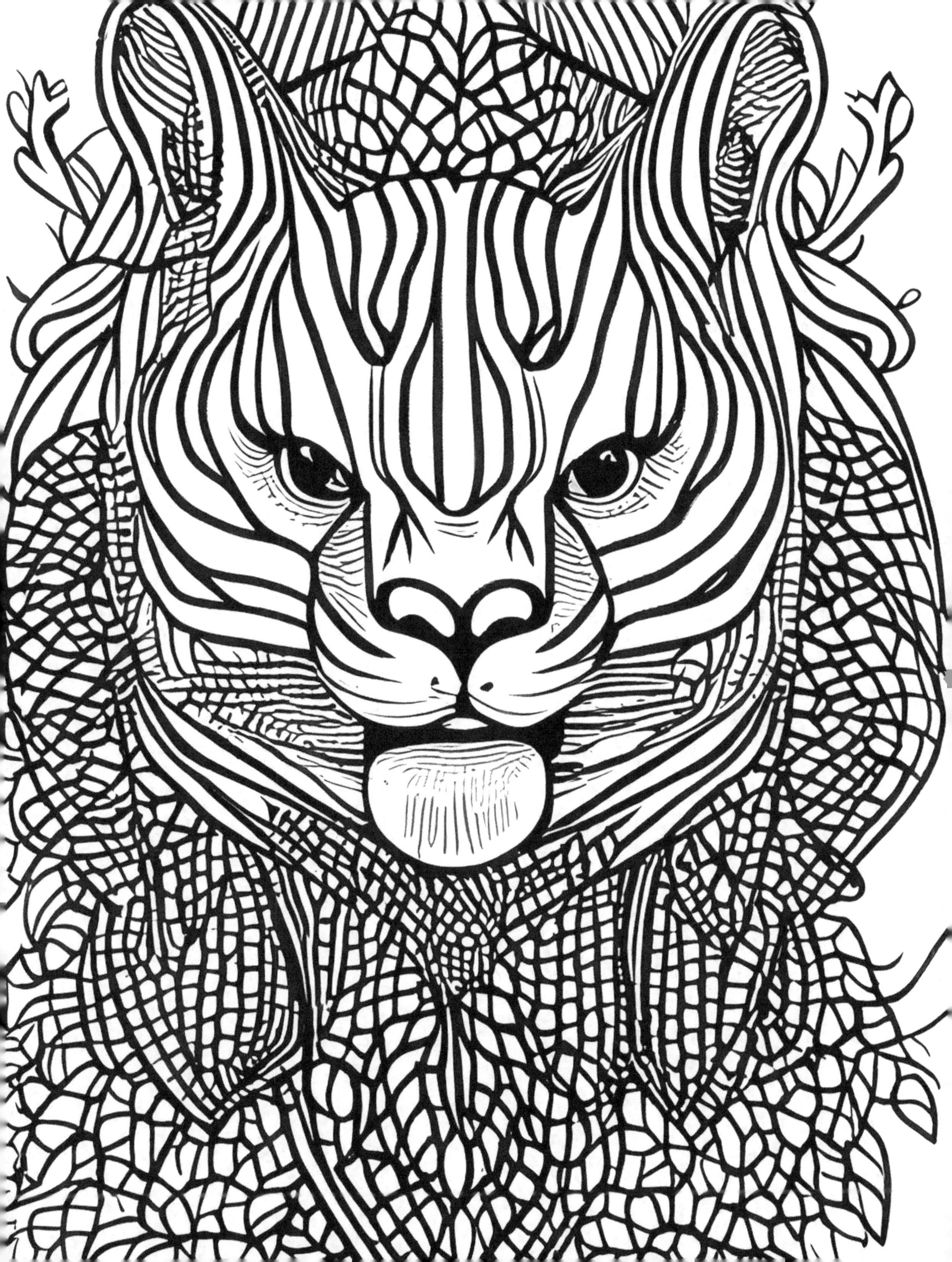

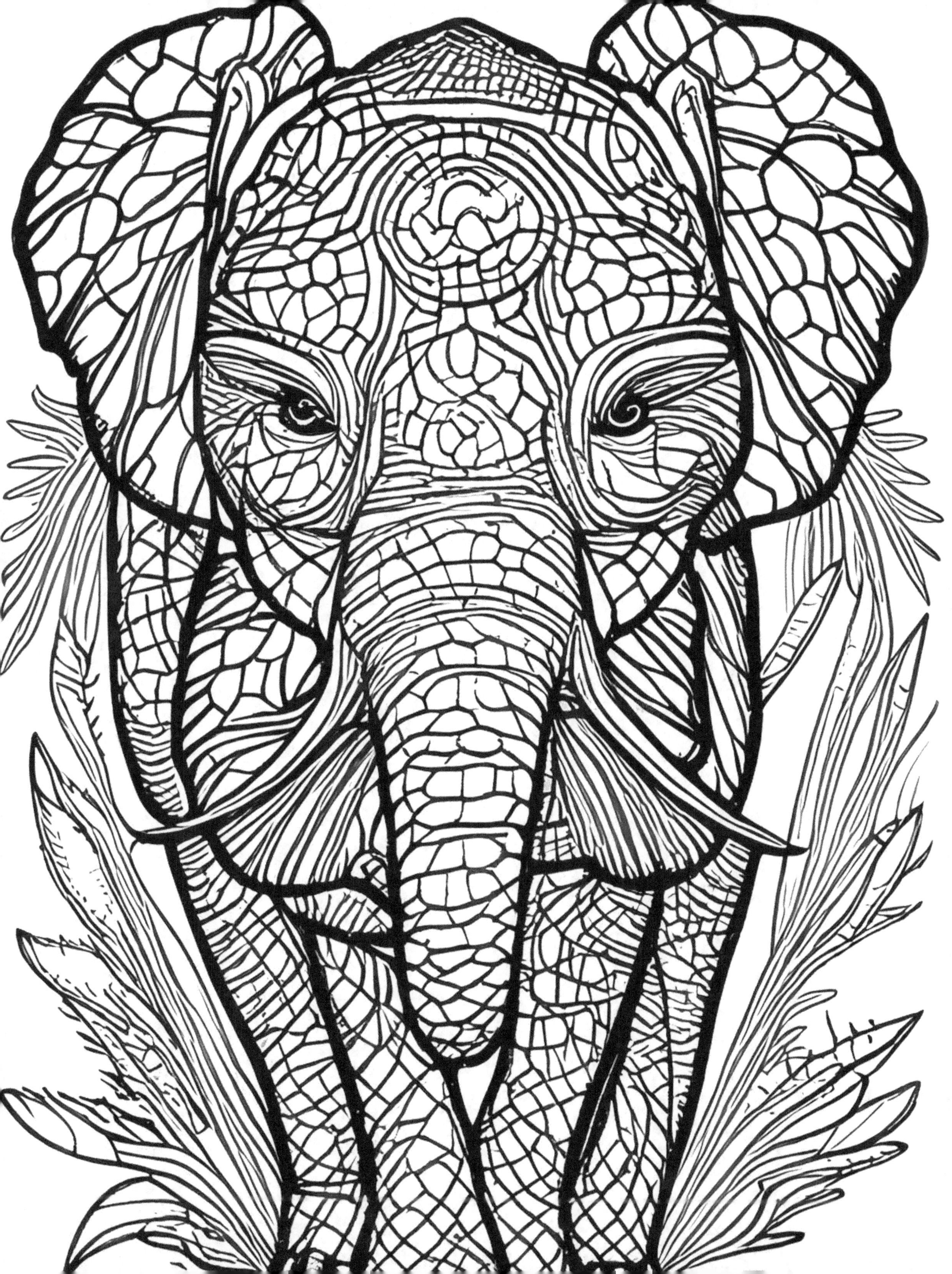

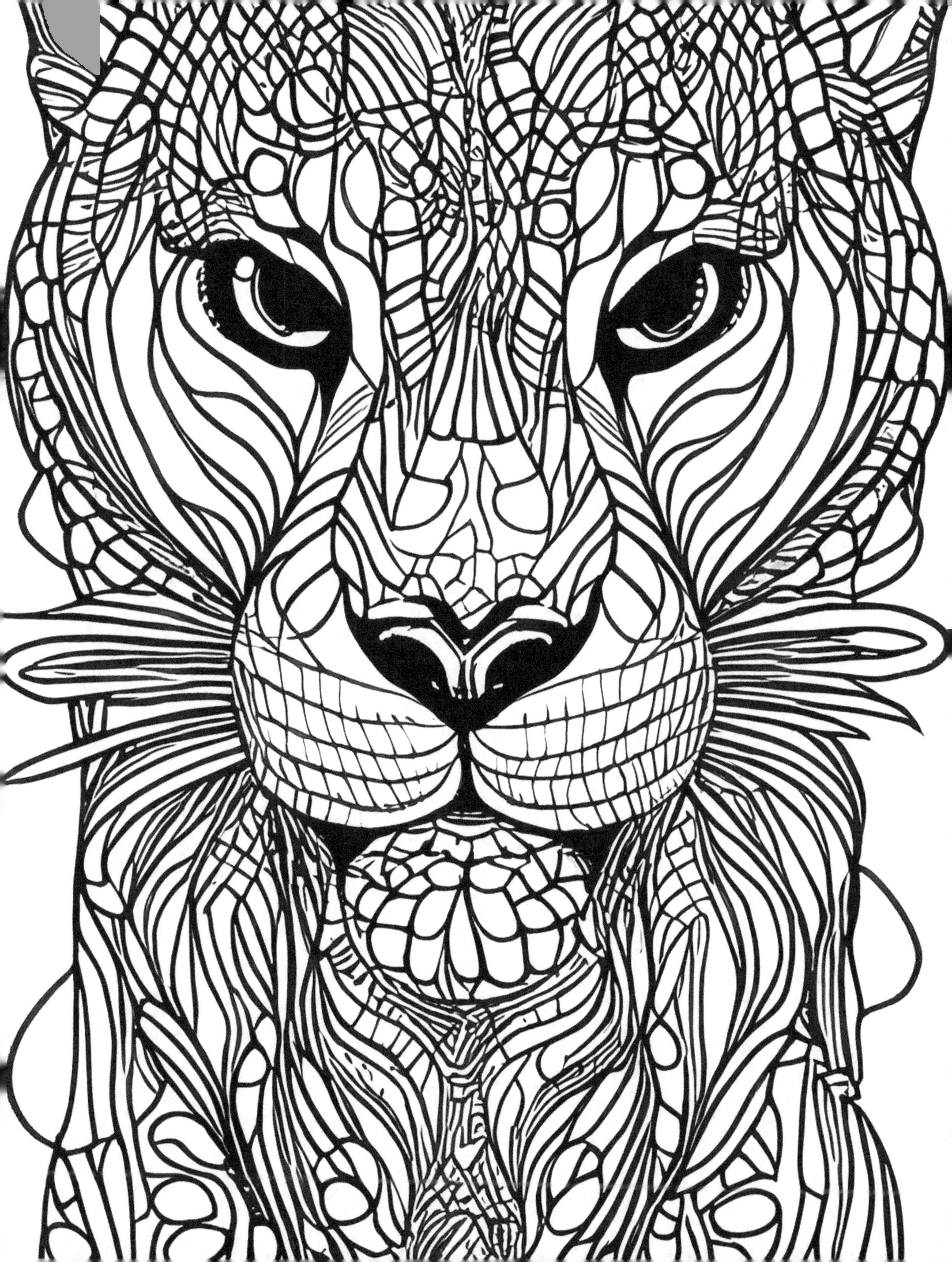

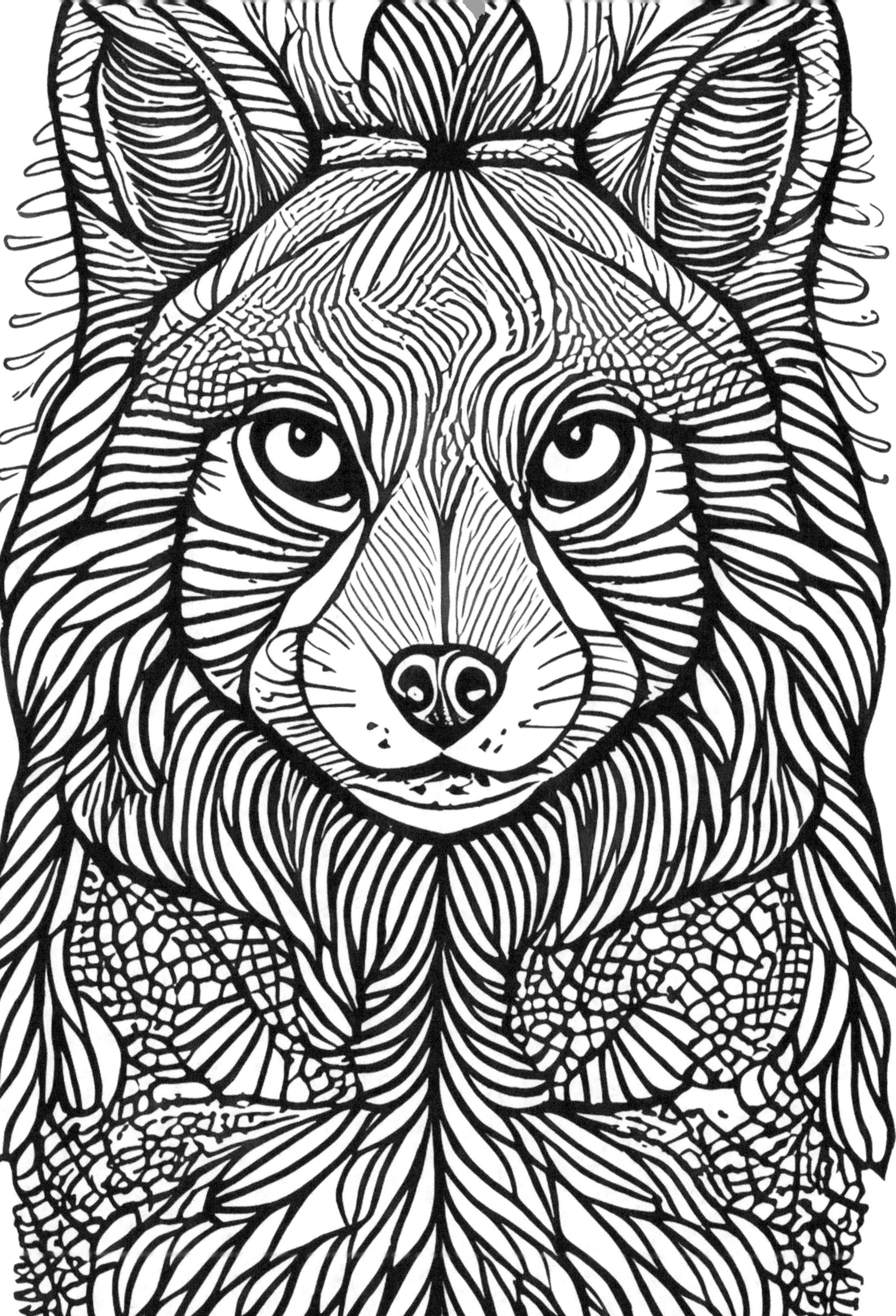

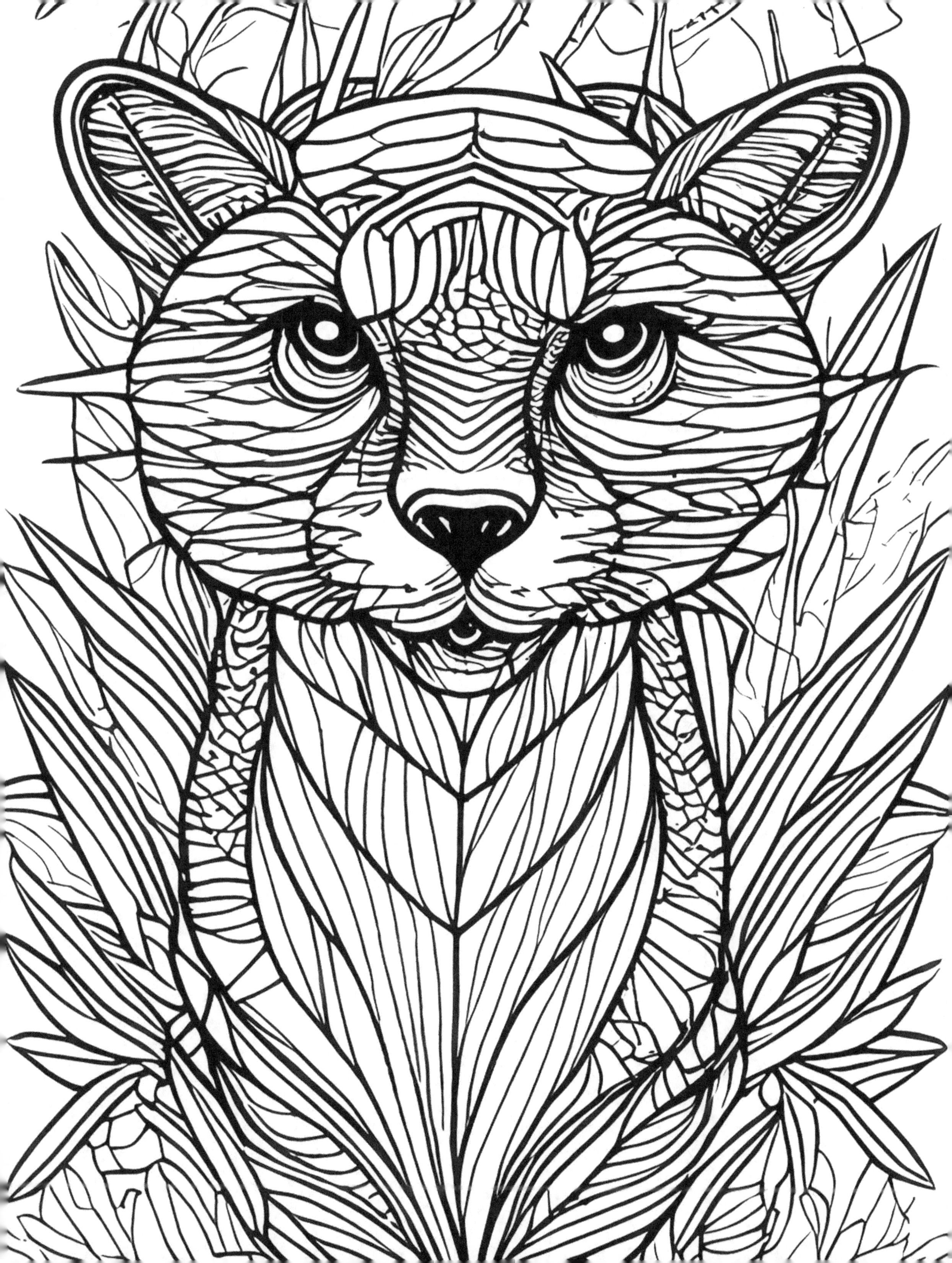

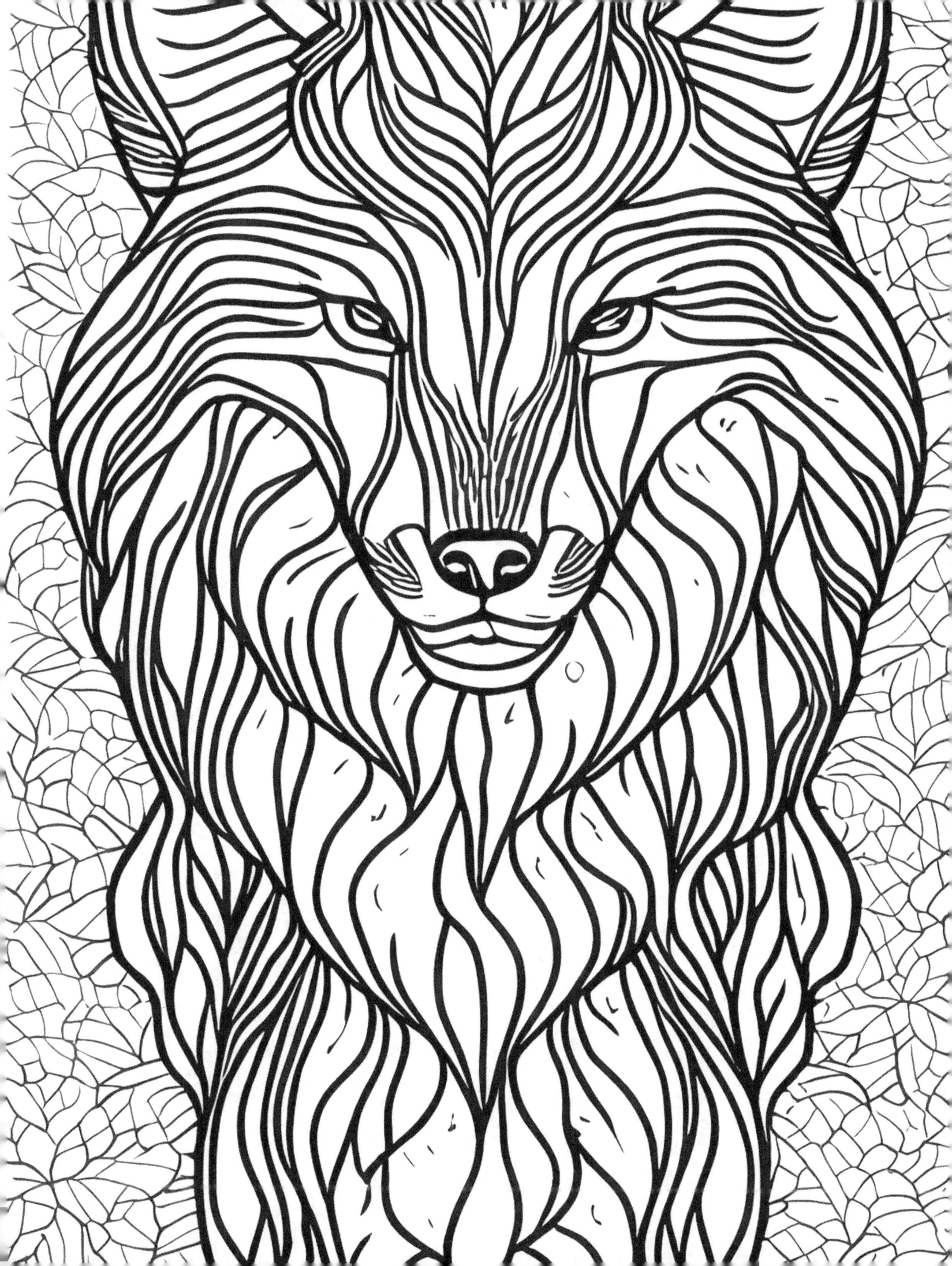

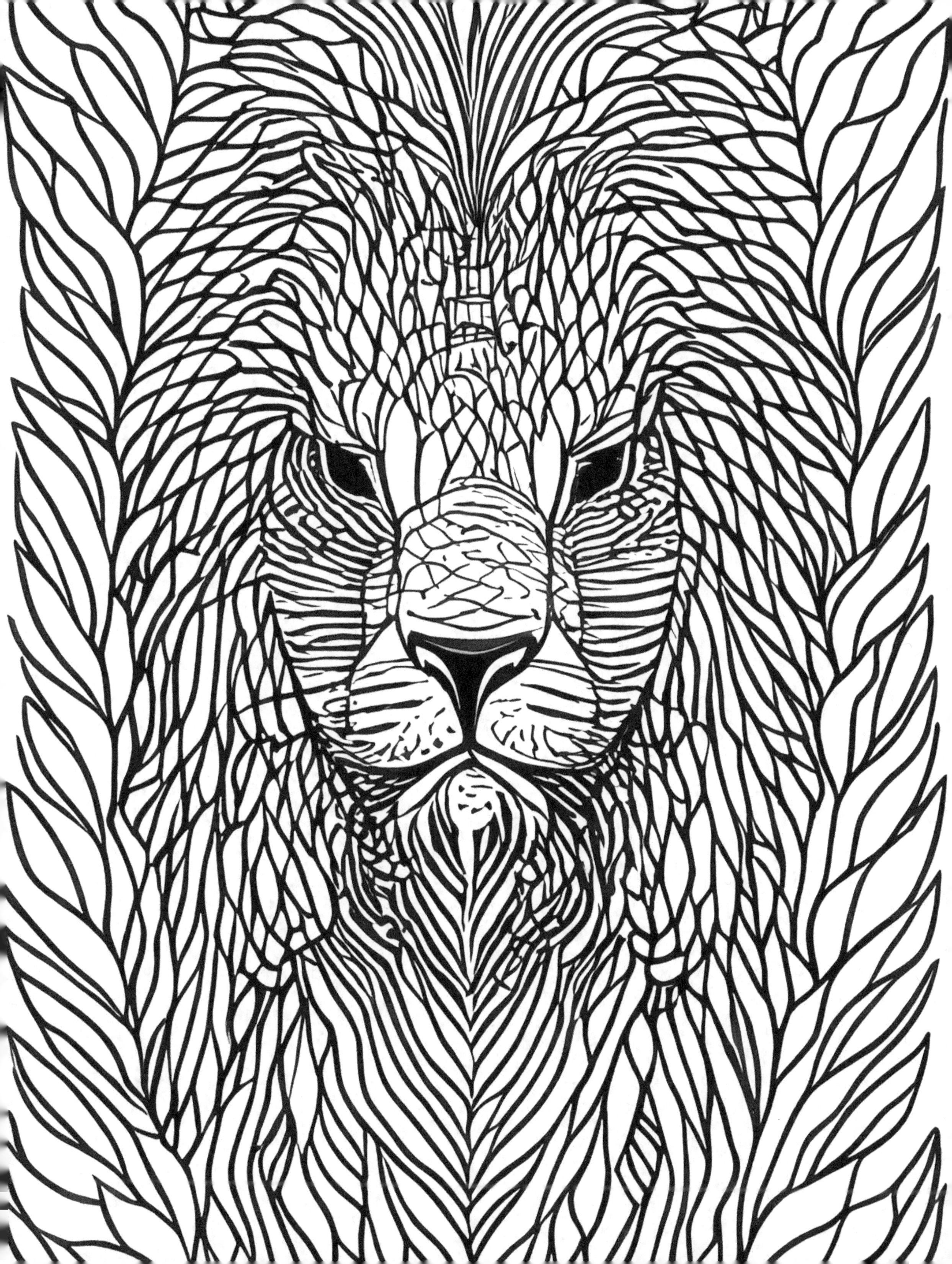

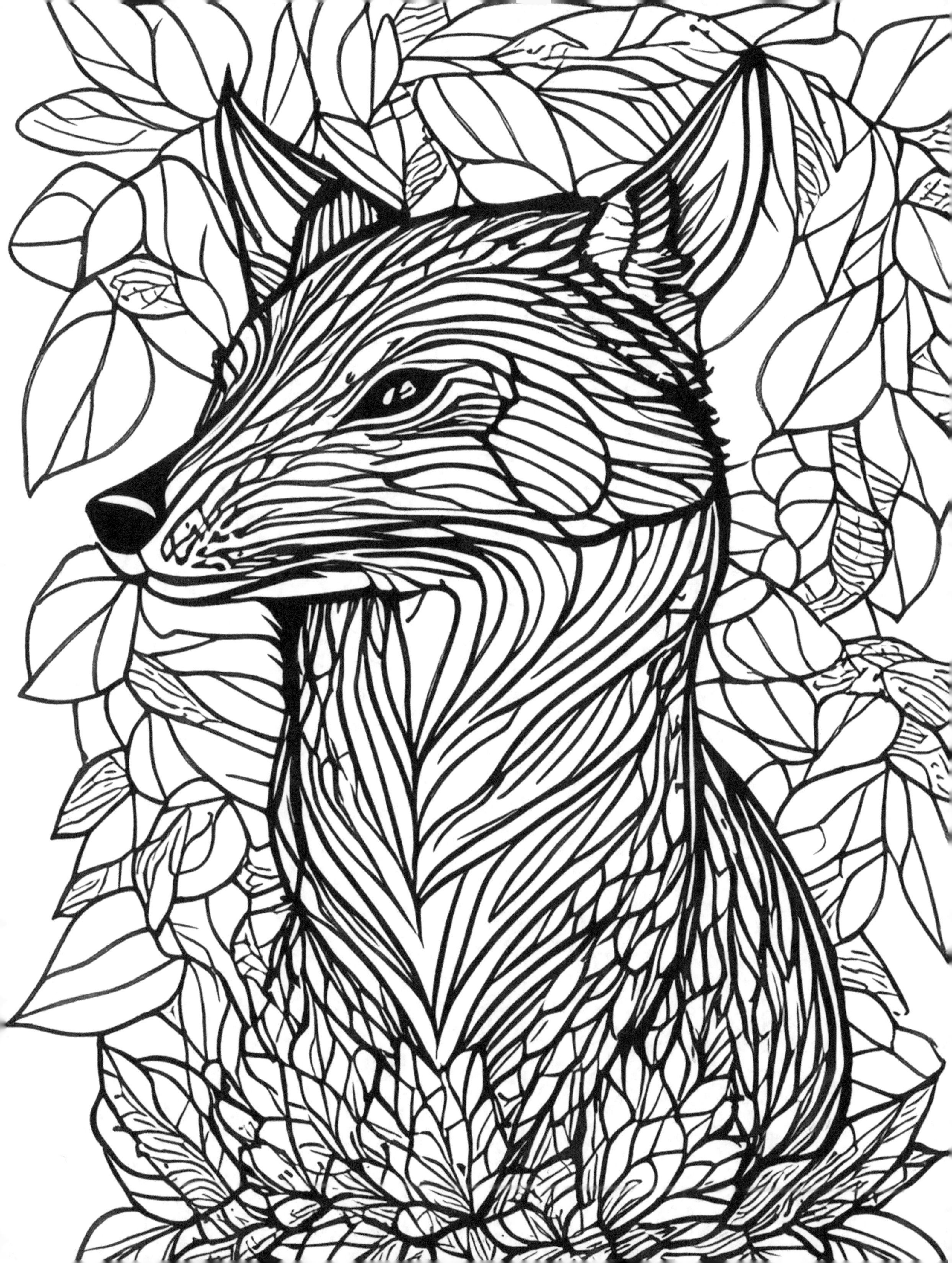

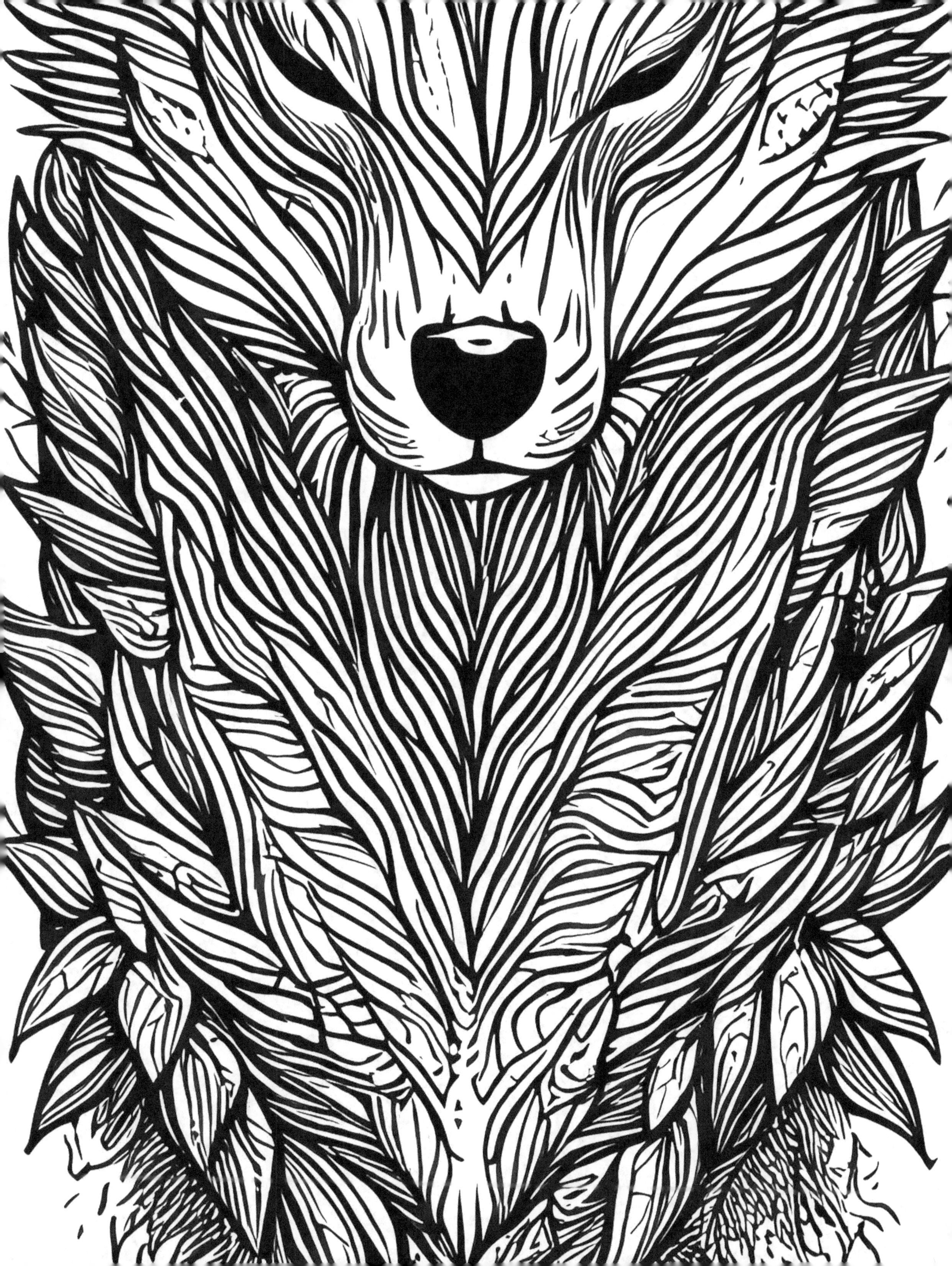

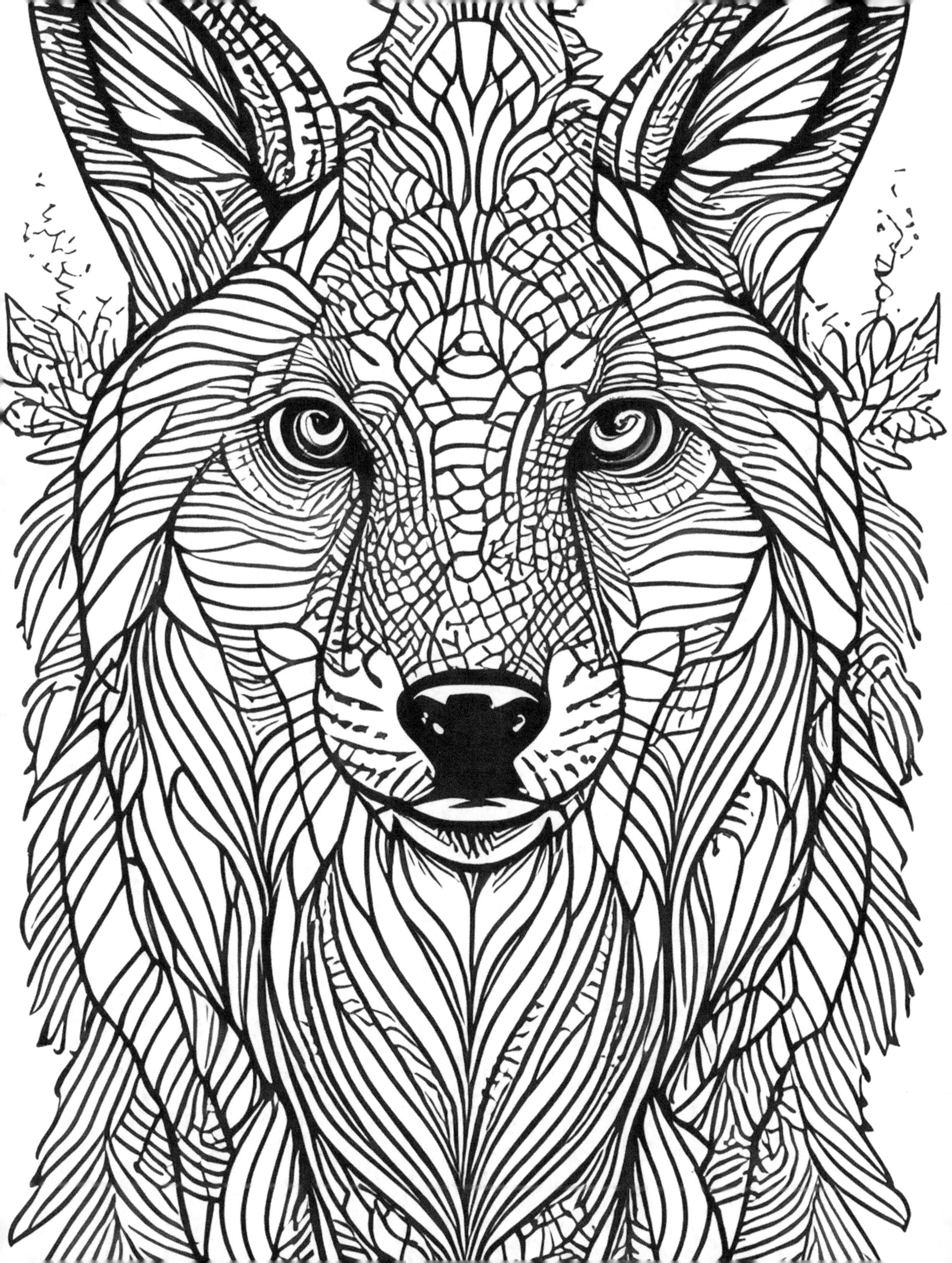

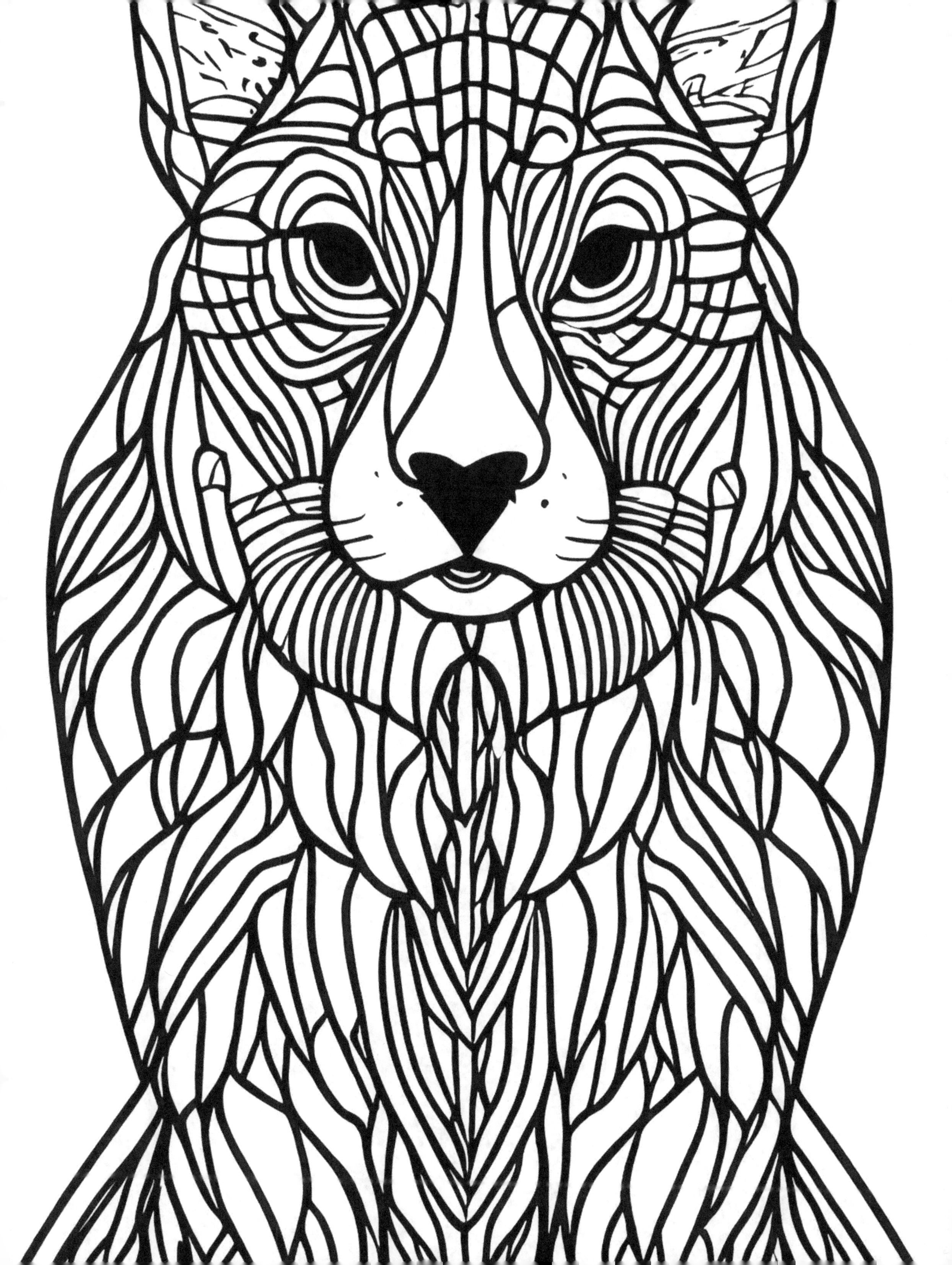

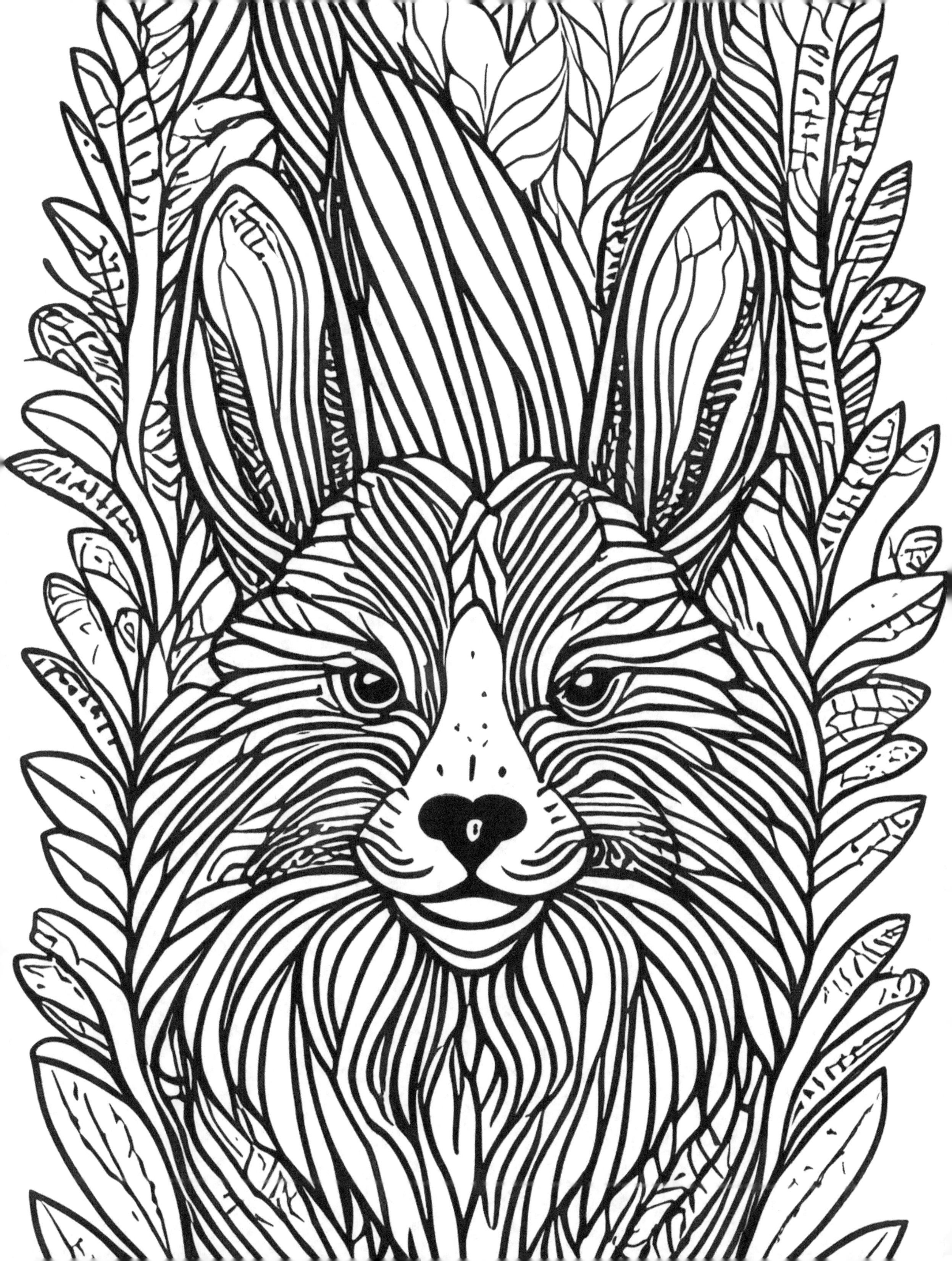

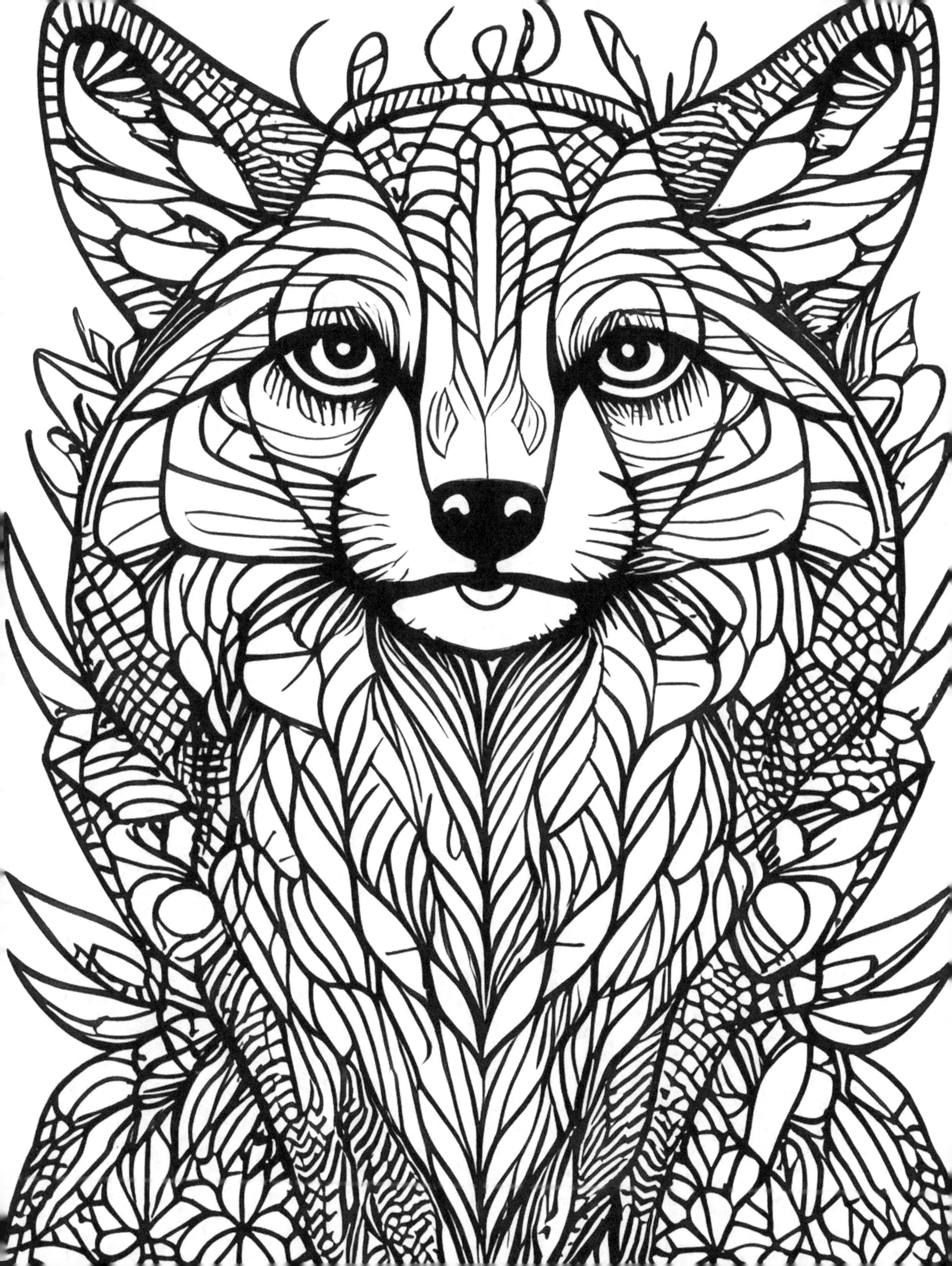

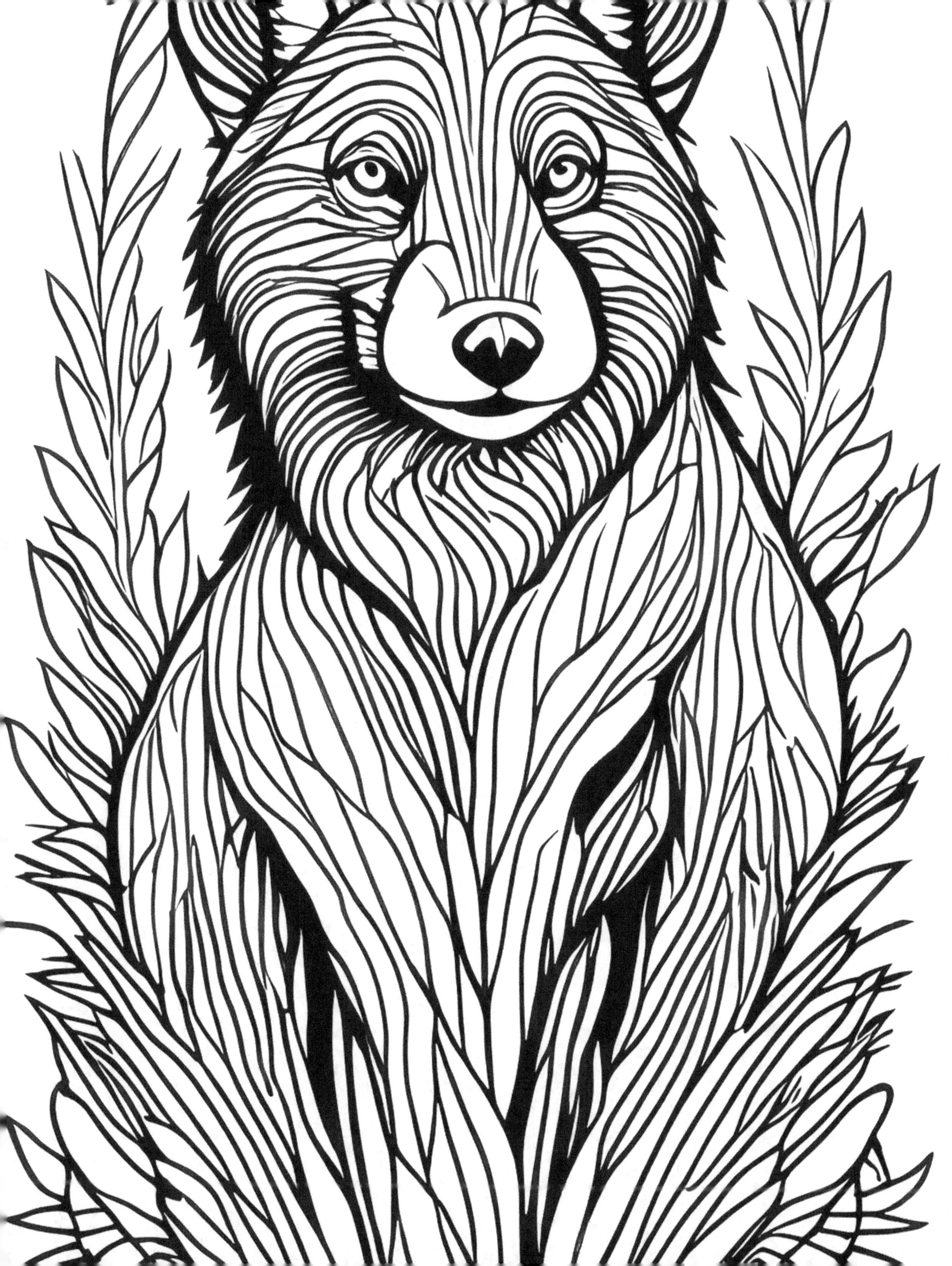

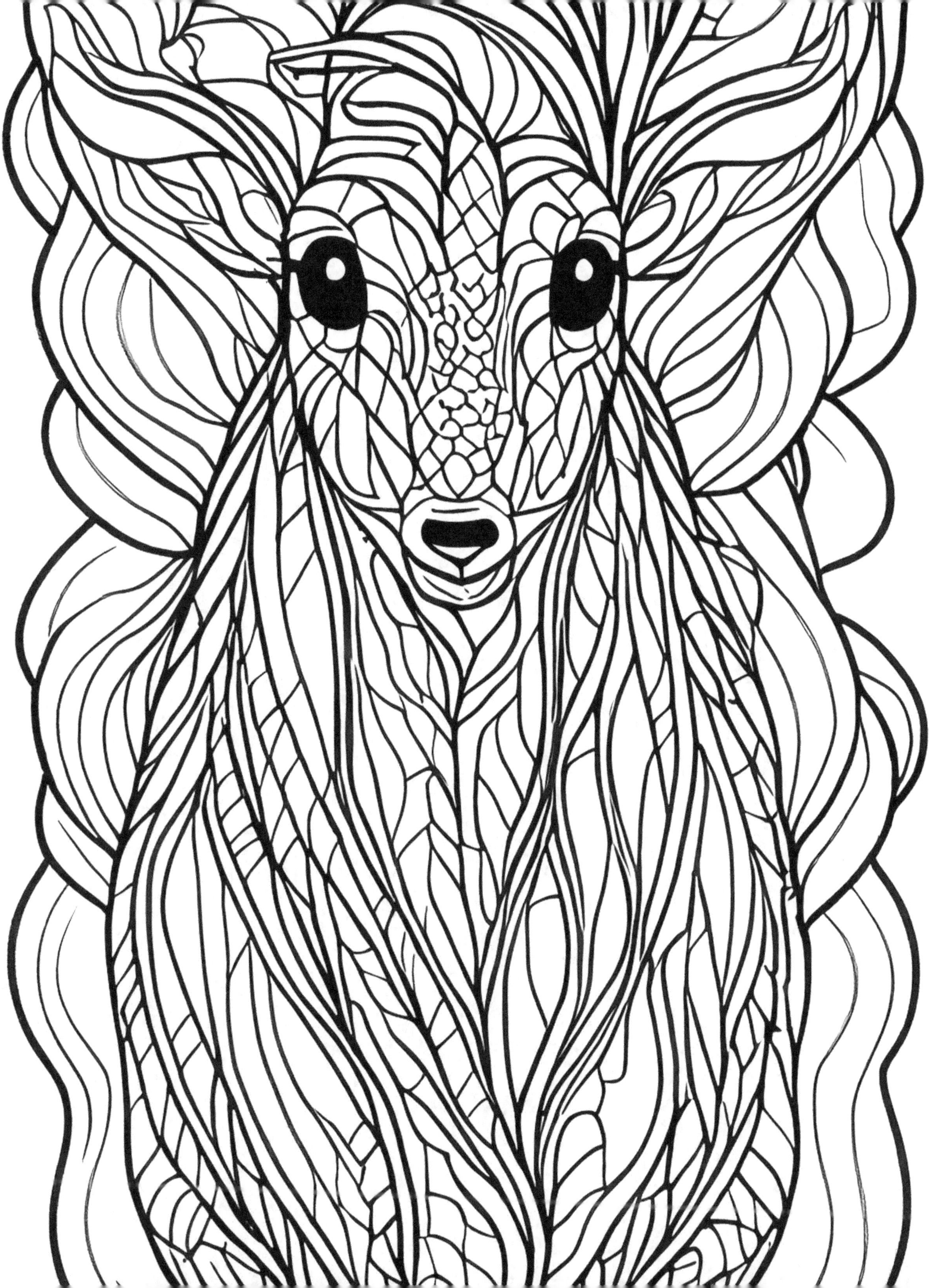

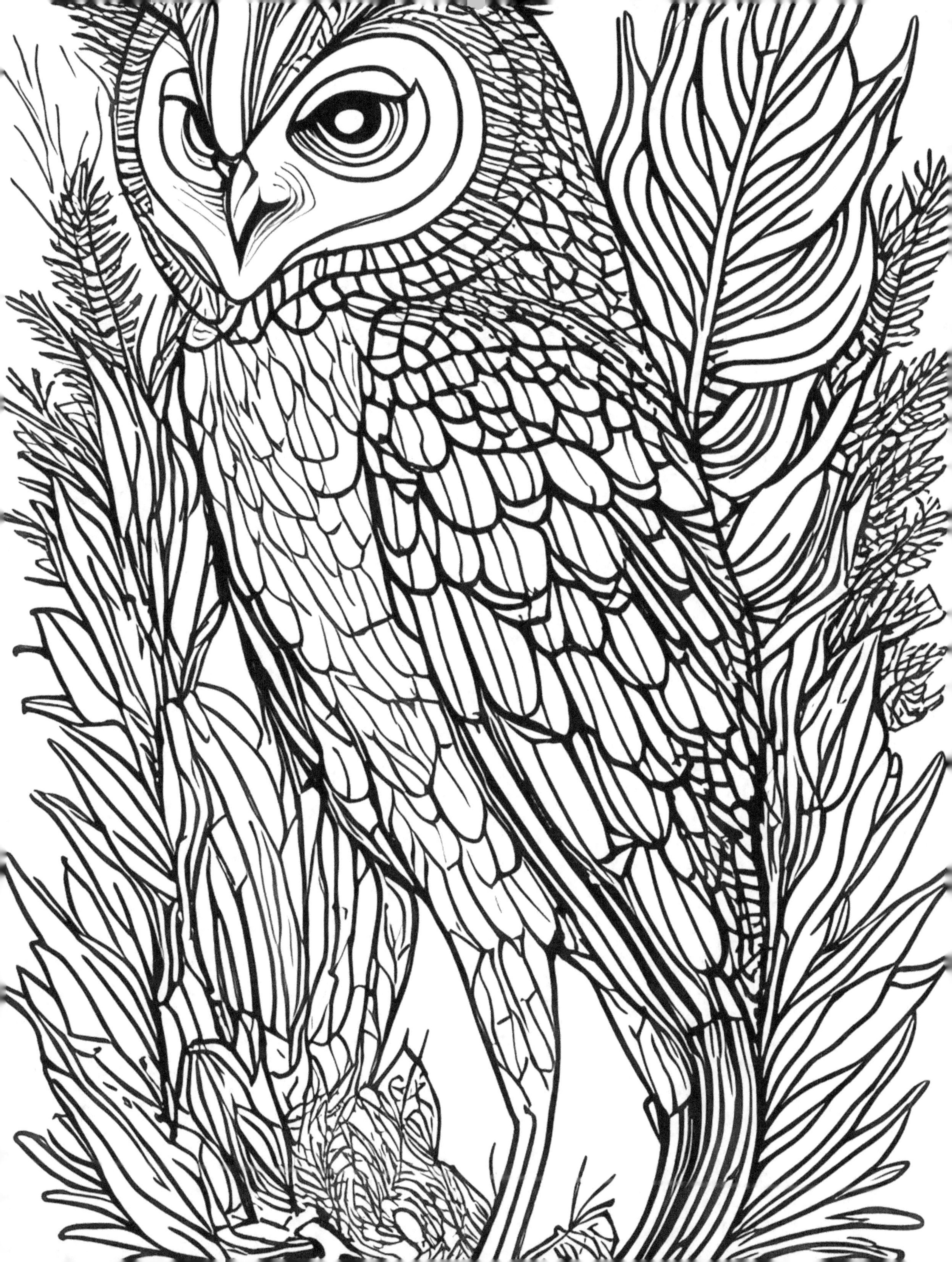

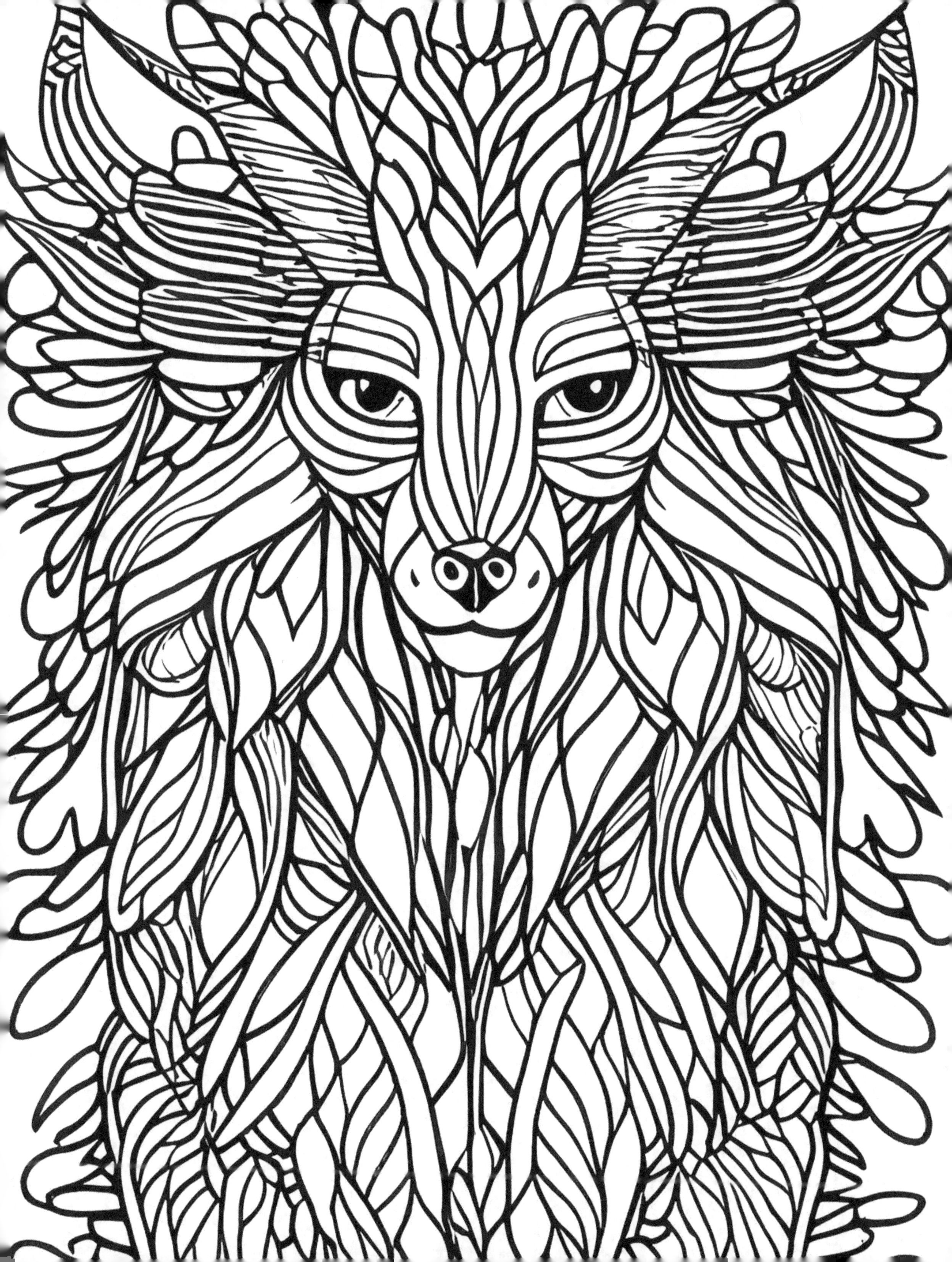

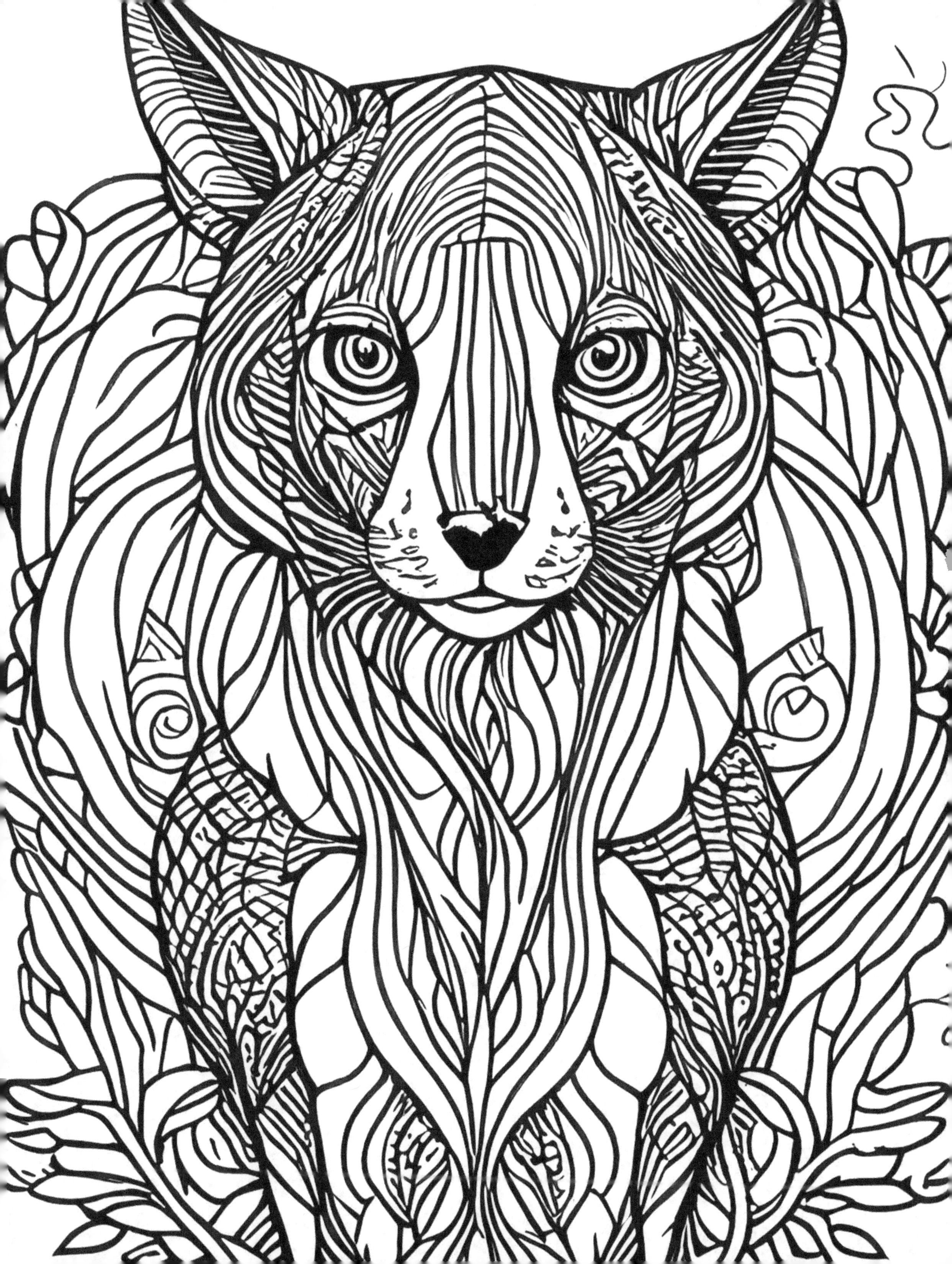

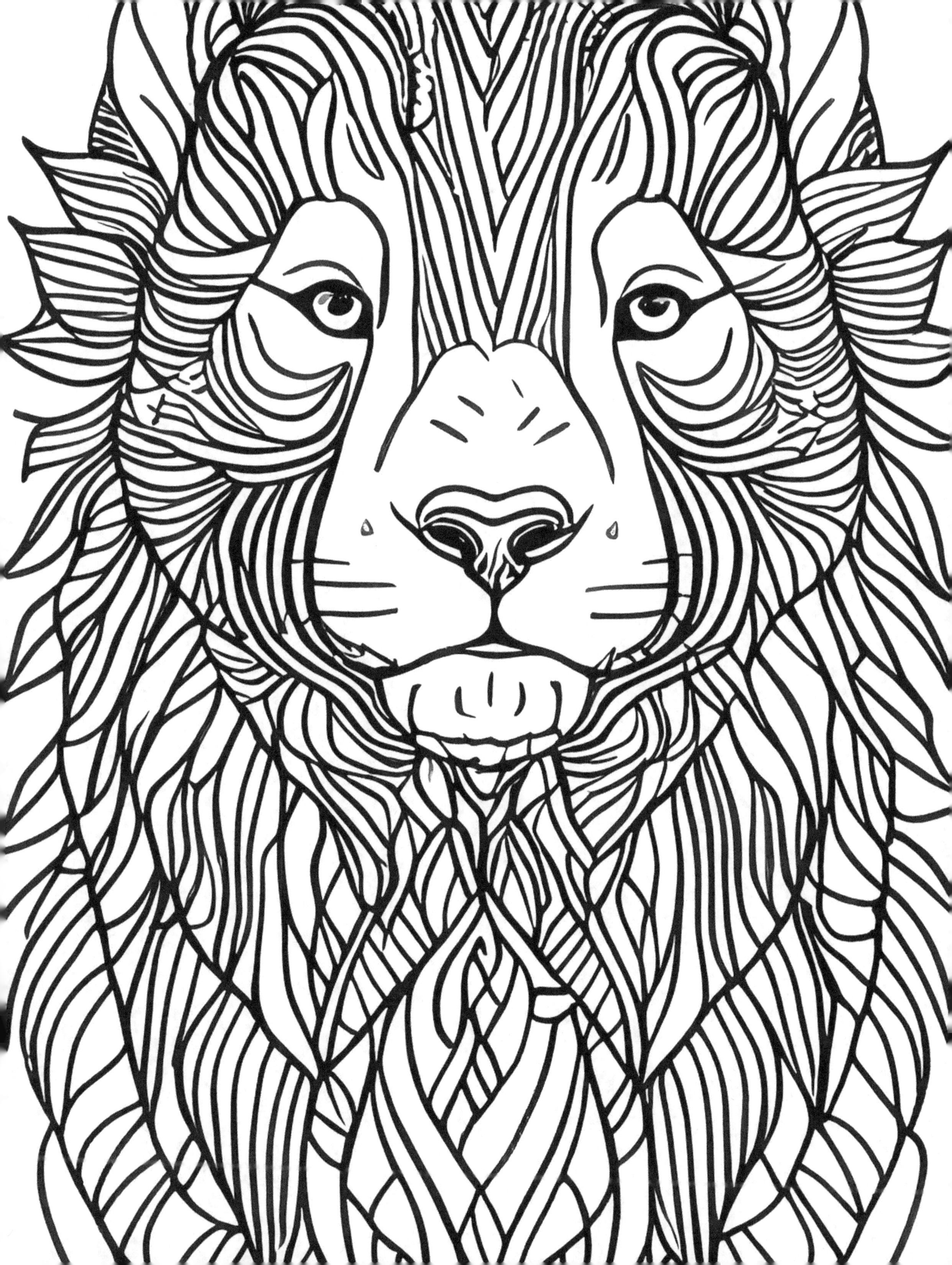

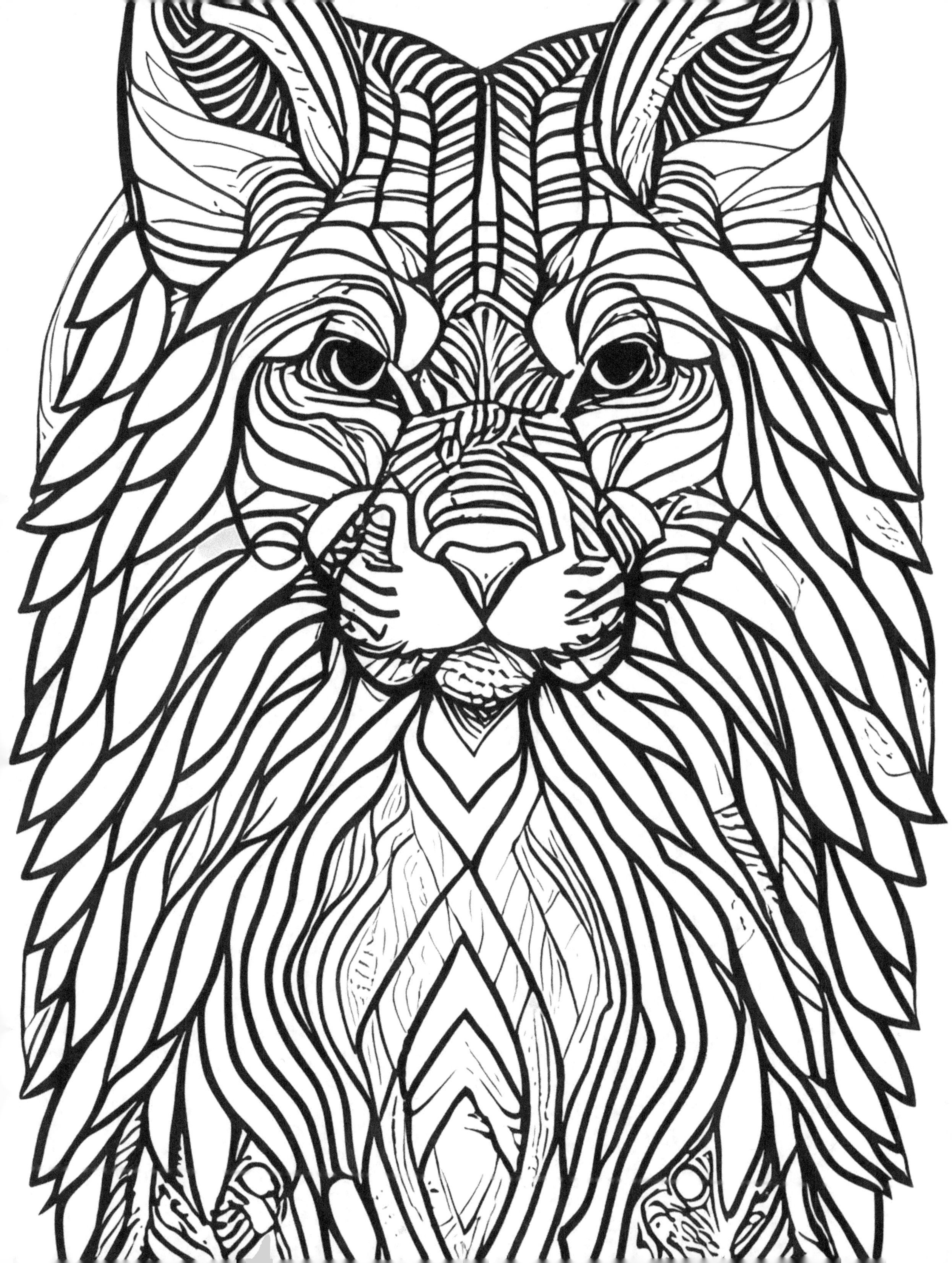

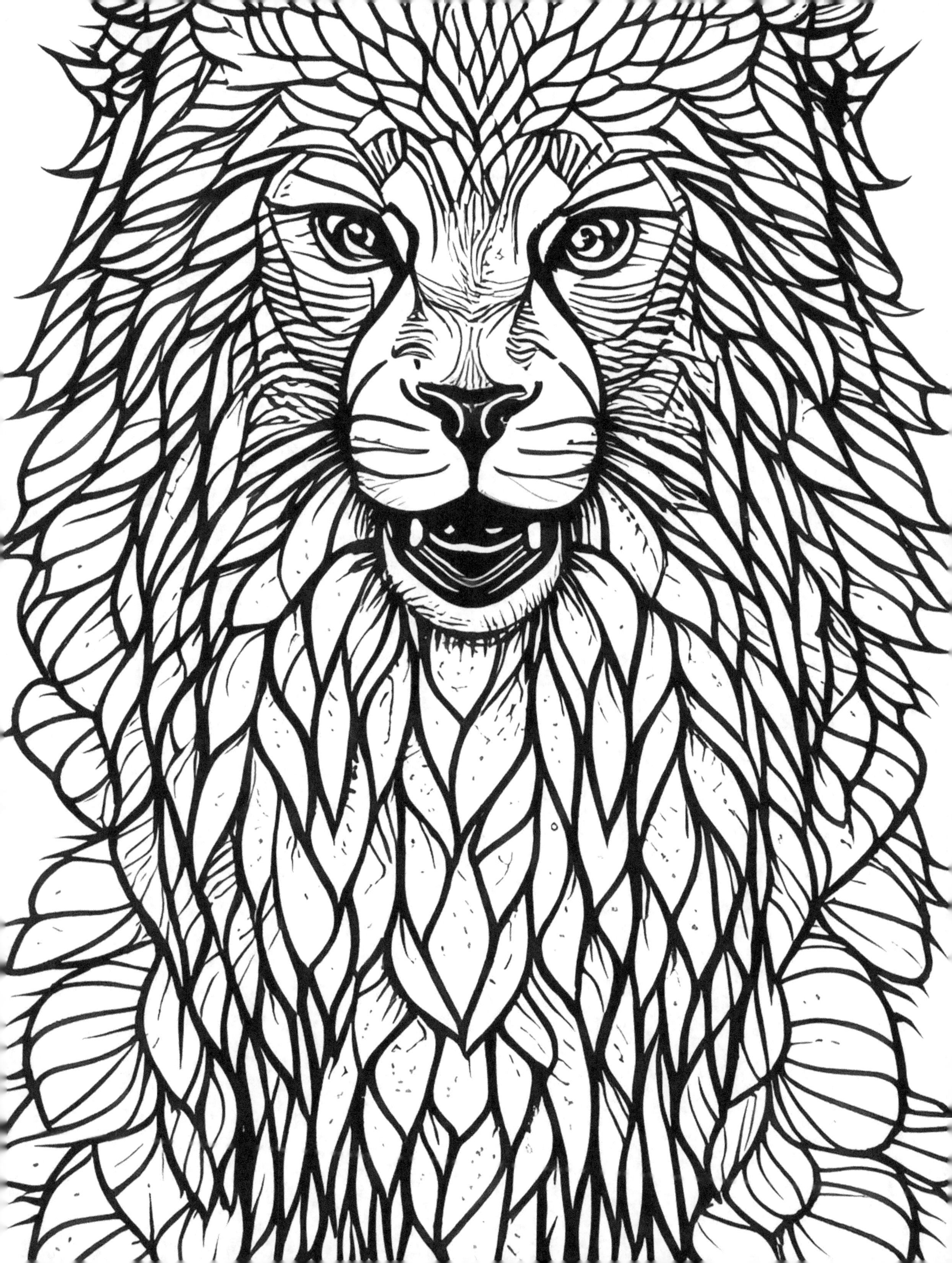

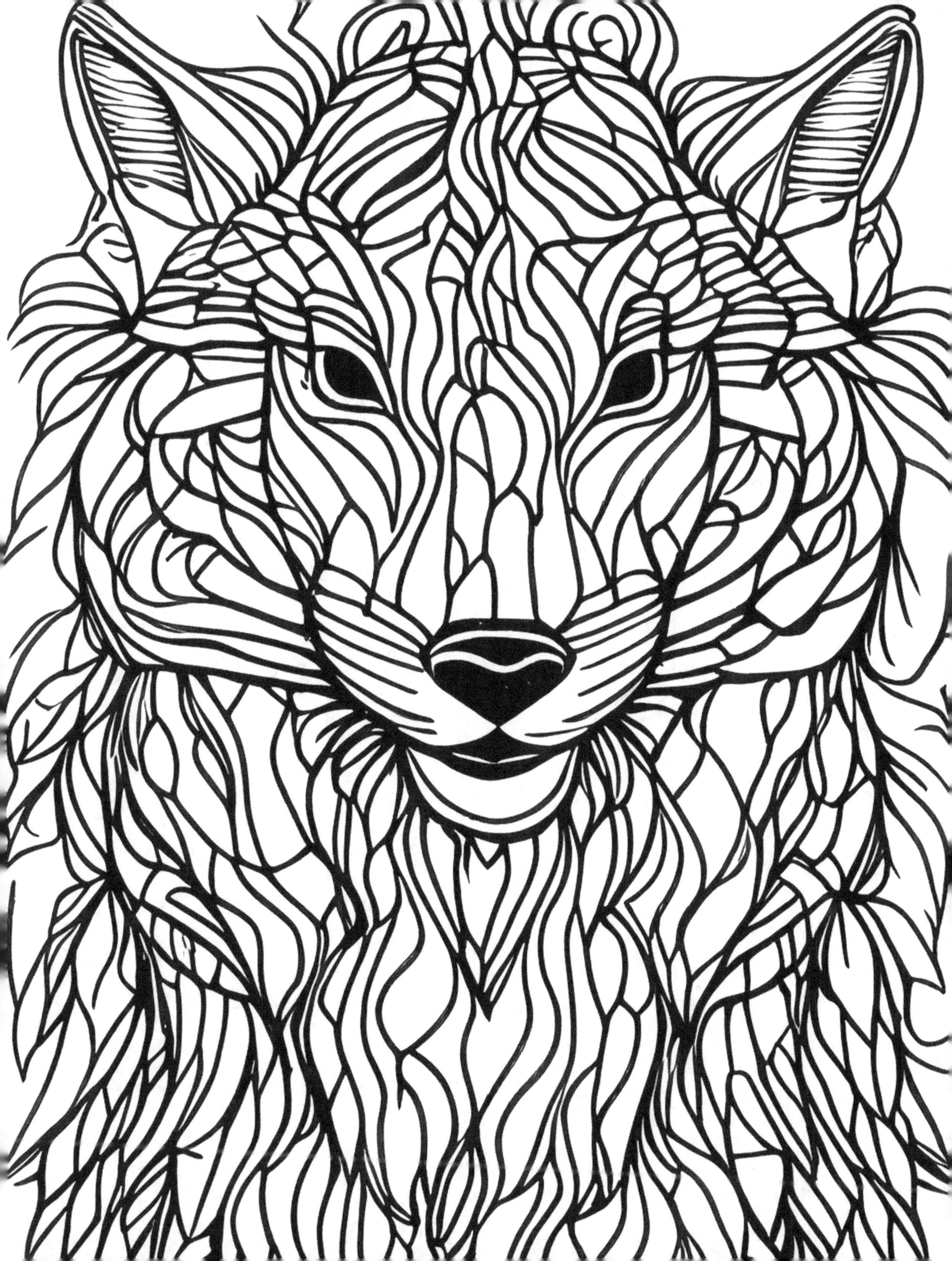

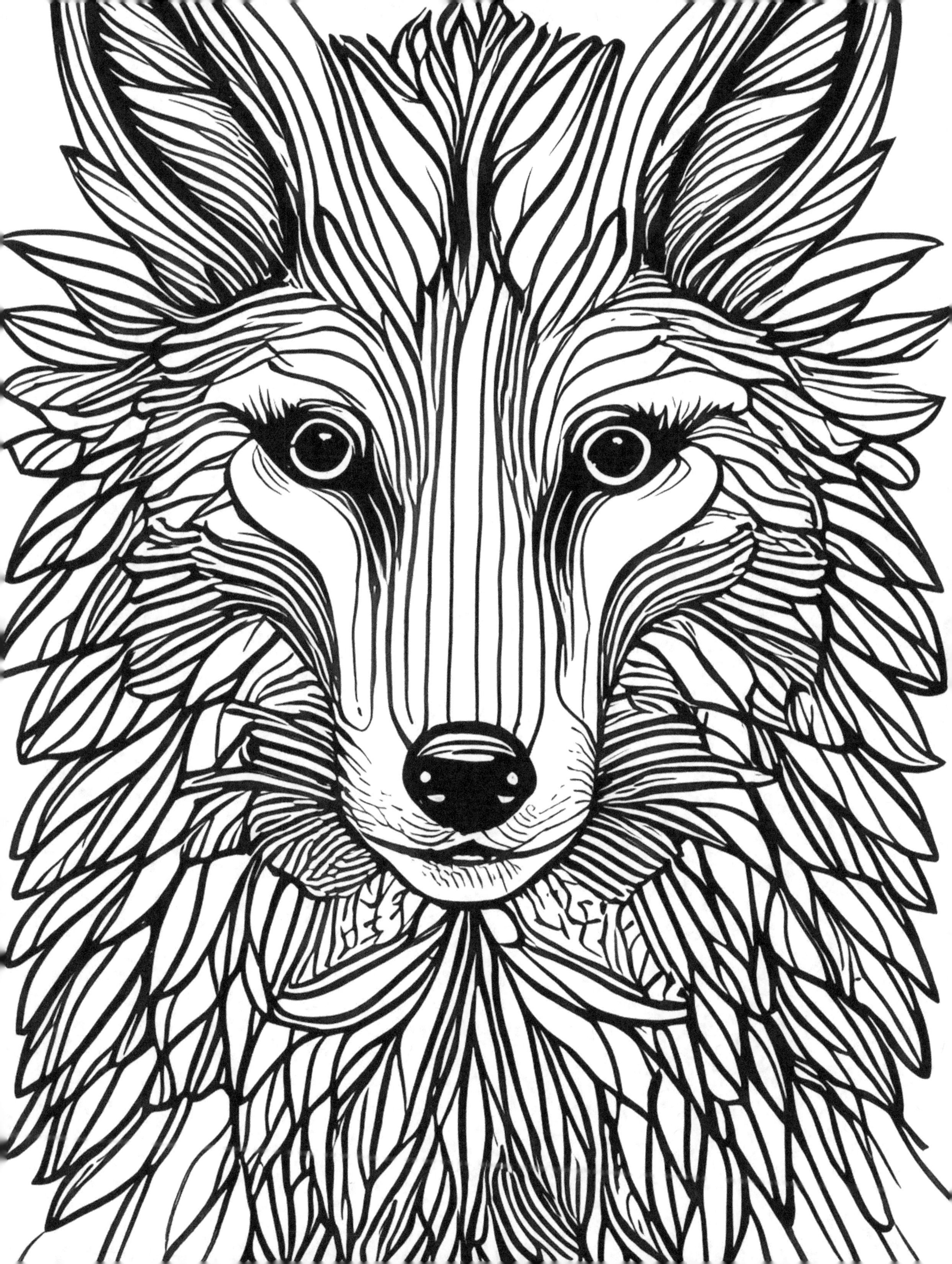

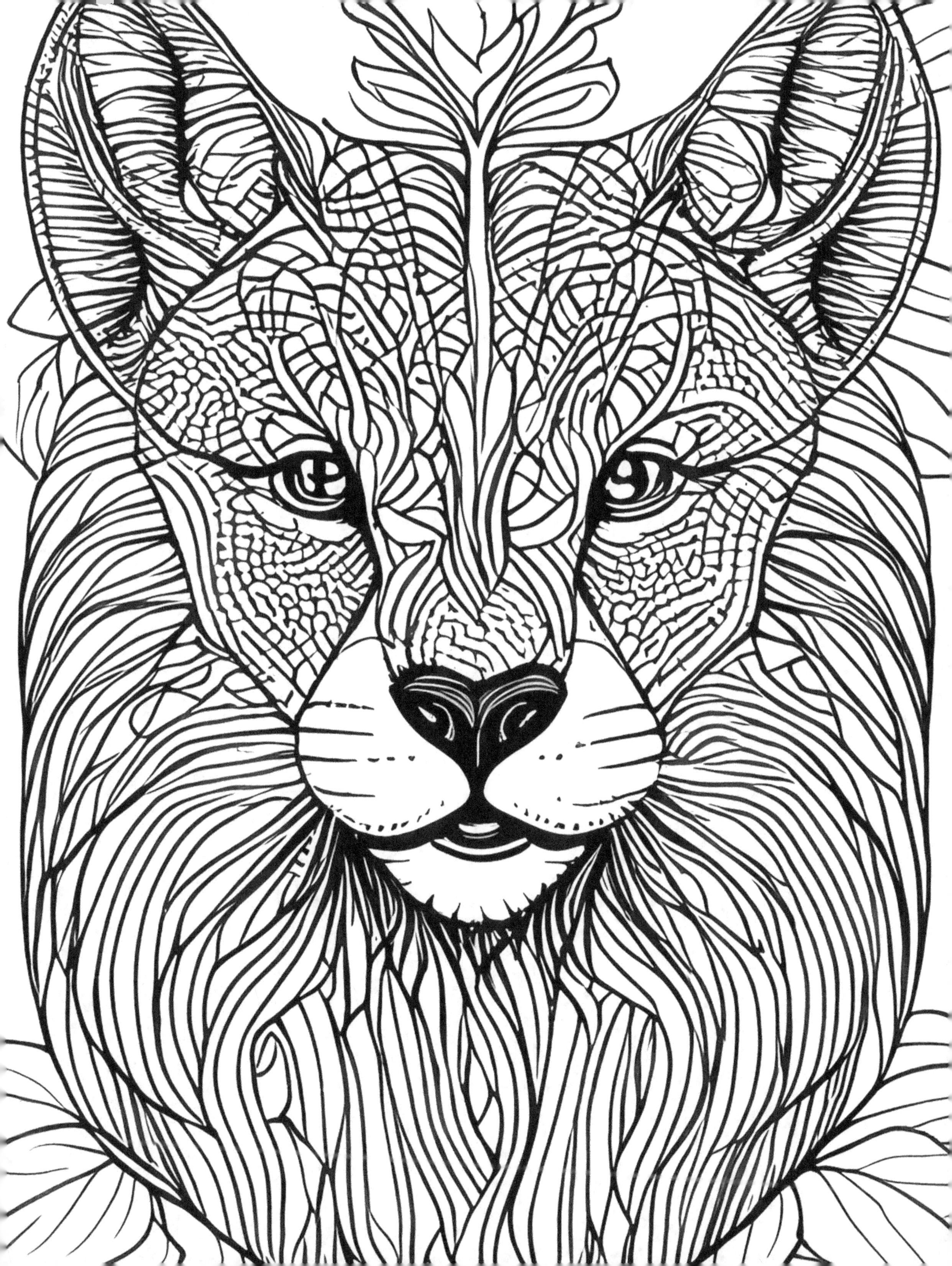

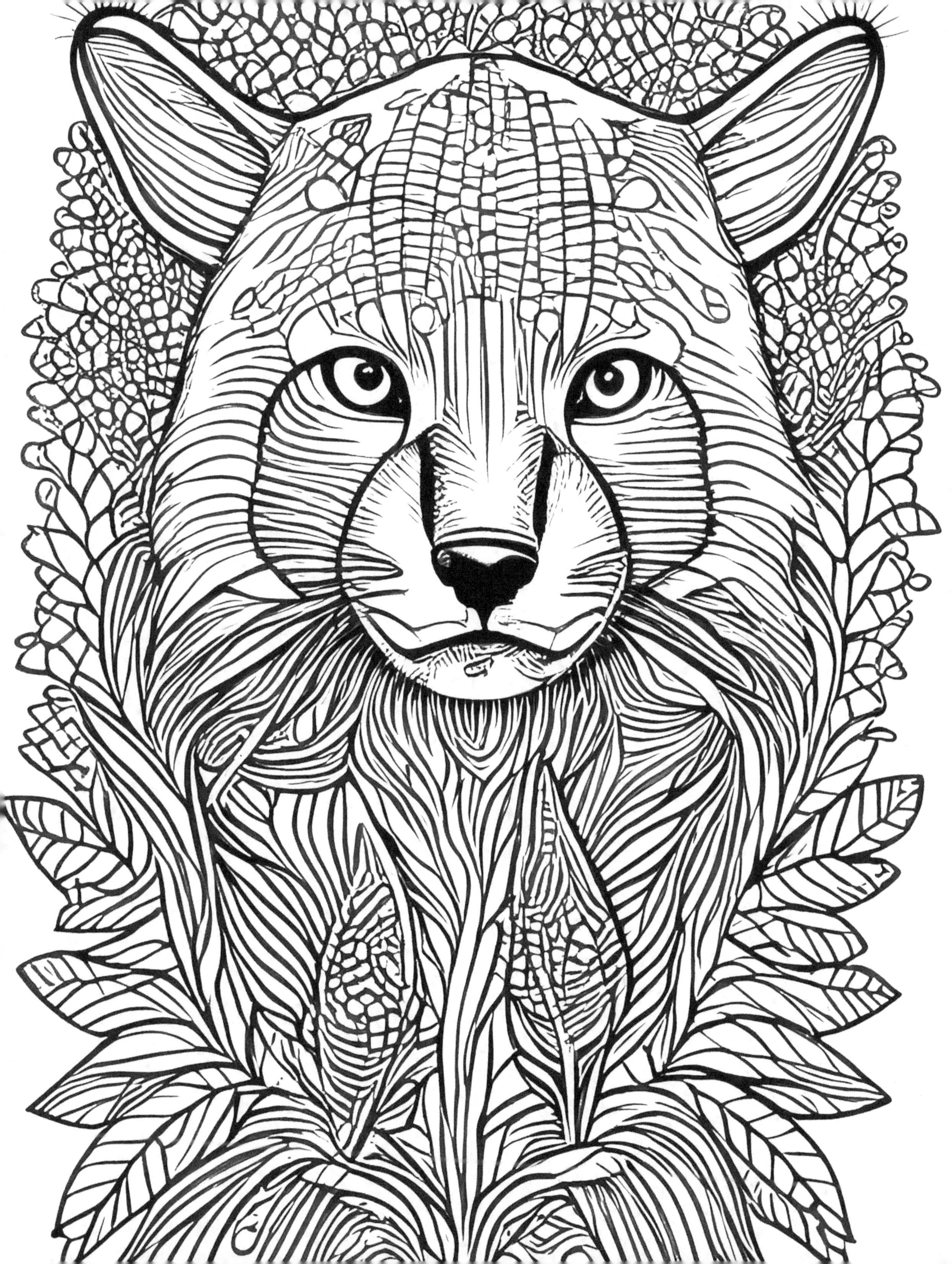

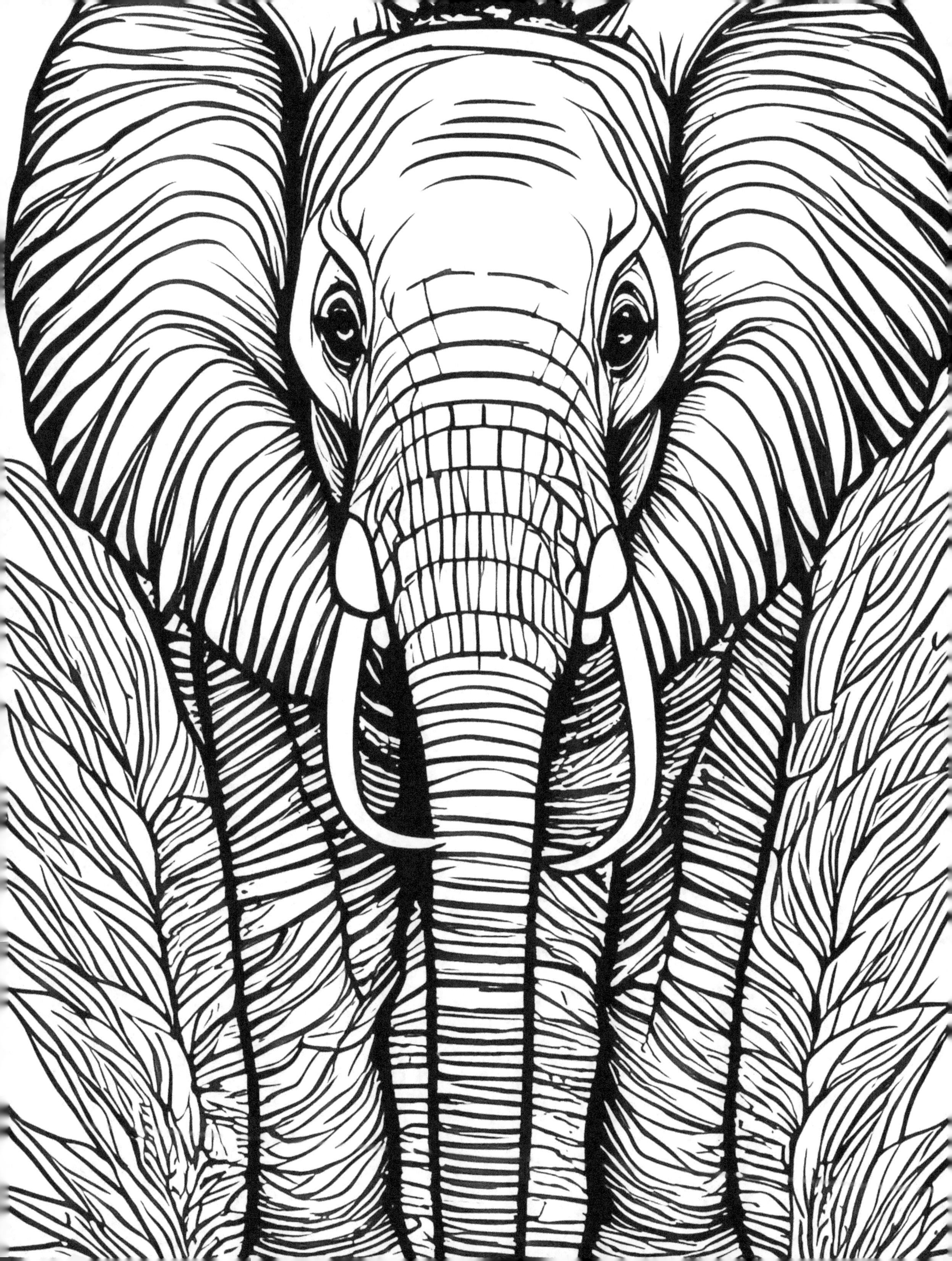

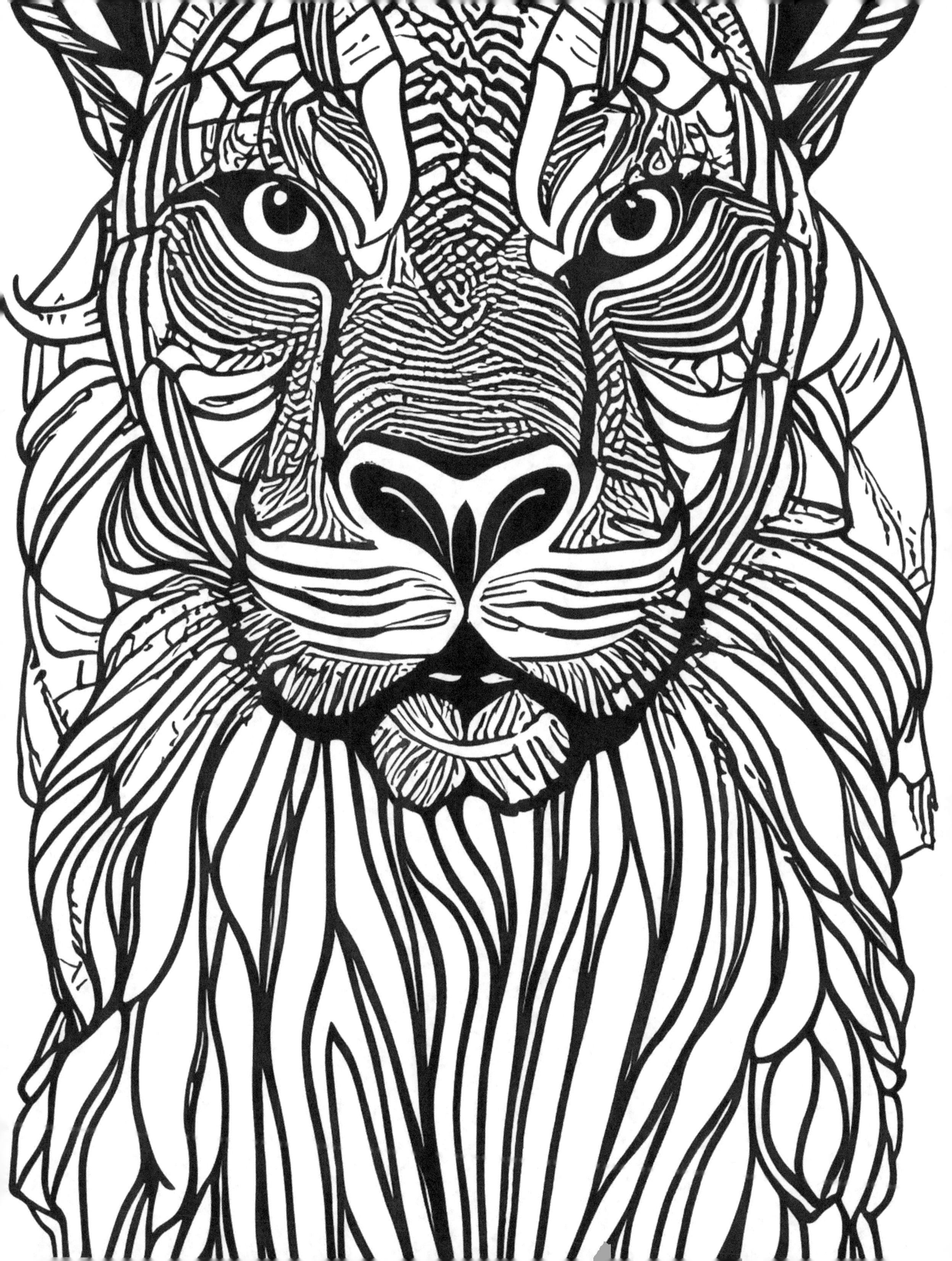

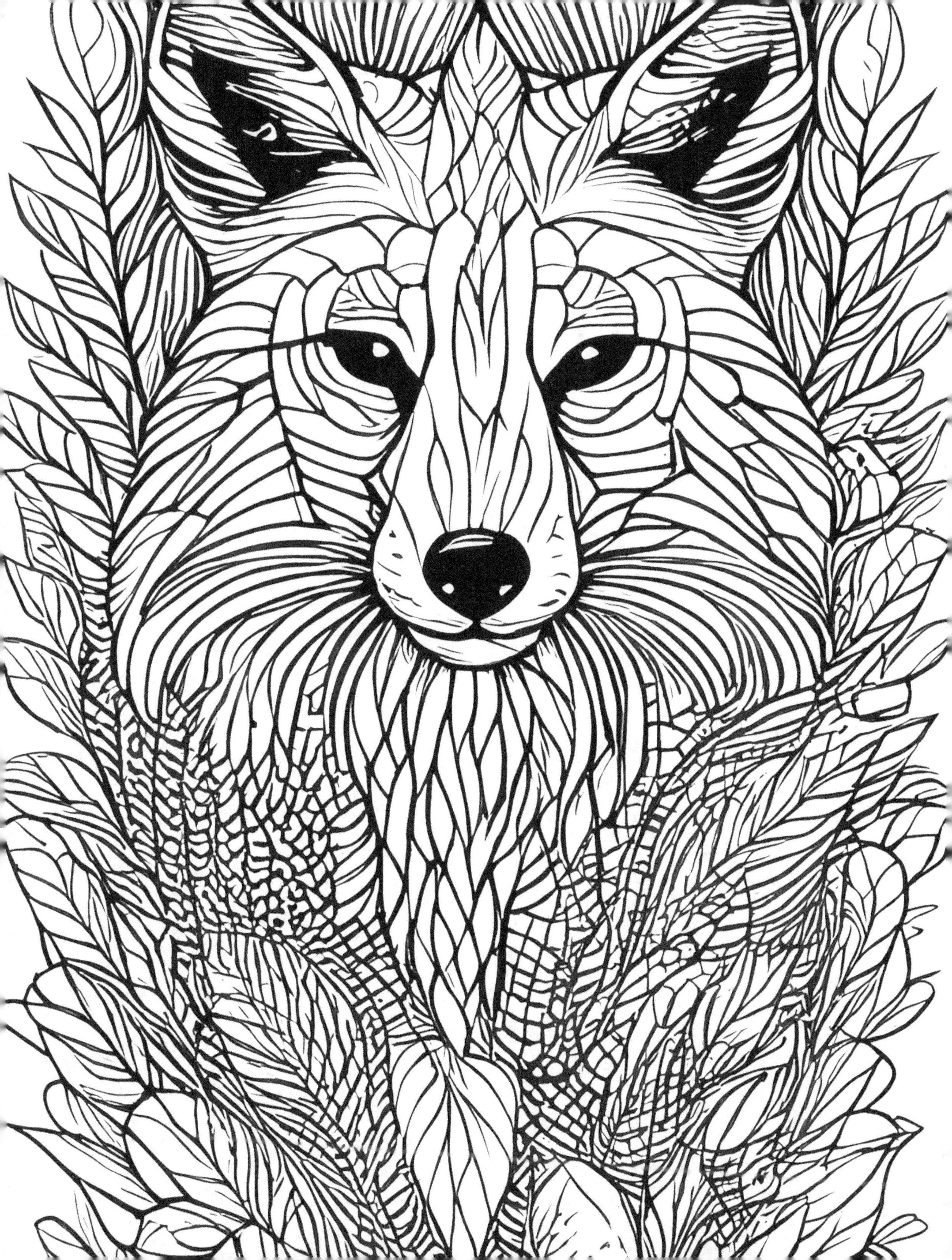

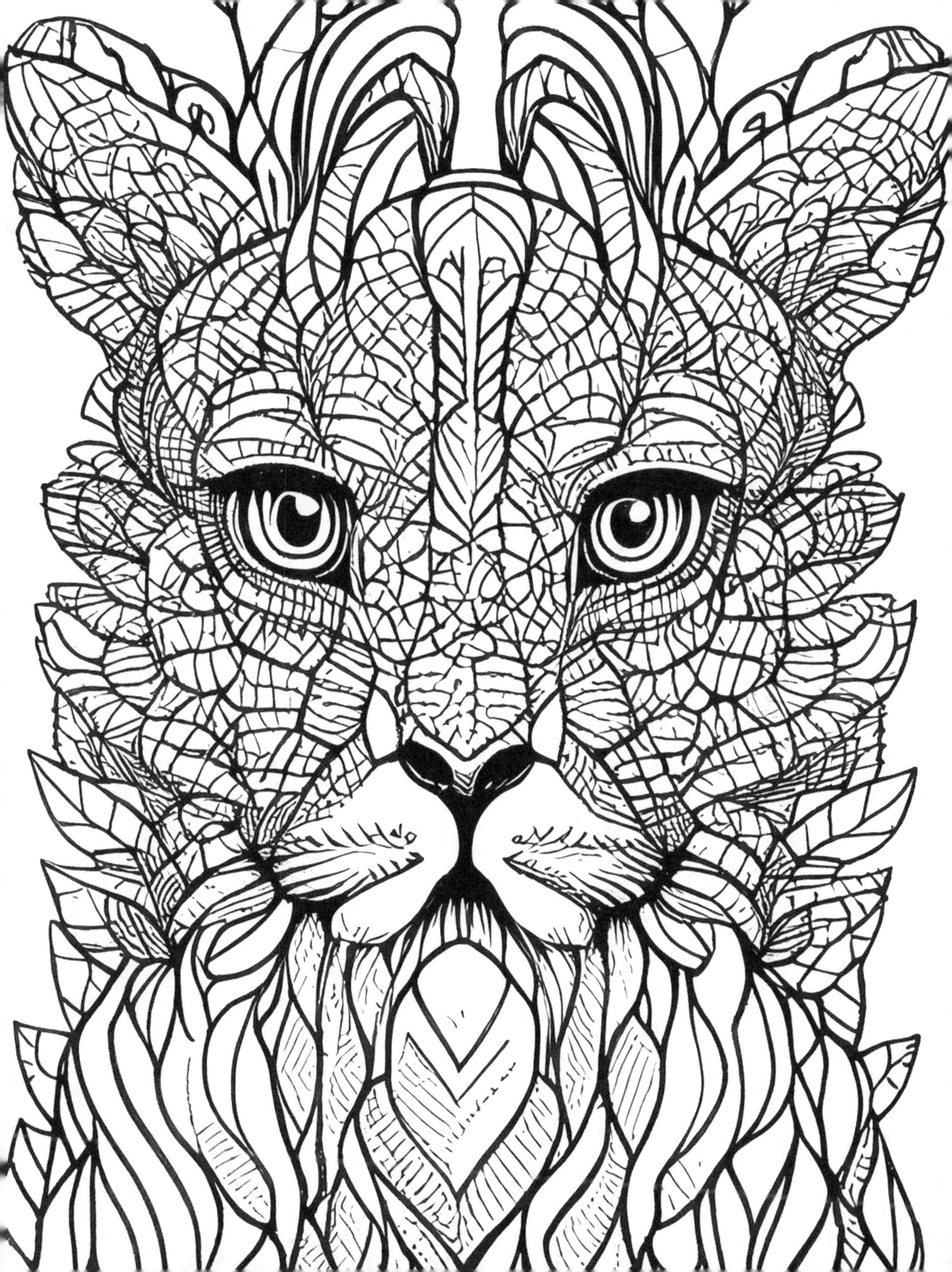

Allpress Publications

Coloring Books on Amazon

www.ingramcontent.com/pod-product-compliance
Lightning Source LLC
Chambersburg PA
CBHW081019240526
45471CB00017B/3419
9798323244010